Basildon Famous People

By

Ken Porter

First published in Great Britain in Paperback in 2016 by

Affinity Self Publishing Ltd

ISBN

Copyright © Ken Porter 2016

The right of Ken Porter to be identified as the author of this work has been asserted by him in accordance with the Copyright, Designs and Patents Act 1988.

Apart from any use permitted under UK Copyright law, this publication may only be reproduced, stored, or transmitted, in any form, or by any means, with prior permission in writing of the publishers or, in the case of reprographic production, in accordance with the terms of licenses issued by the Copyright Licensing Agency.

A catalogue record for this book is available from the British Library.

Affinity Self Publishing Ltd
www.affinityselfpublishing.co.uk
info@affinityselfpublishing.co.uk

Basildon Famous People

Contents	Page
Author	5
Acknowledgements @Contributors	6
Introduction	7
Chapter 1 The Puritans	8
The Mayflower – Christopher Martin	8
Hugo Peters	16
Elizabeth Reade (The Reade Family)	20
Chapter 2 Various	26
Rev. John Pell - Priest	26
Nathaniel Woodard - Educationalist	31
Dr. Henry Selby Hele-Shaw – Engineer/Inventor	36
Edgar Longstaffe - Artist	39
Cecil Hewett - Archaeologist	41
Marion Wilberforce – Flying Ace	47
Keith Chapman – Can he fix it	53
Chapter 3 Entertainment	56
Joan Sims - Actress	56
Joe Goodman - Comedian	61
Joan Dowling - Actress	67
Genevieve Alison Moyet - Singer	70
Denise Van Outen – Actresss/Presenter	73
Josh Dubovie - Singer	76
Ernest Longstaffe – Producer & Composer	79
John Georgiadis - Conductor	82
Greg Smith - Producer	87
Graham Kendrick – Modern worship music	90
Richard George Tovey - Actor	95
Lee Martin Evans - Comedian	96
Ireen Sheer - Singer	99
Graham Bonney - Singer	101
Depeche Mode -	107

Vince Clarke	108
Andrew Fletcher	110
Martin Gore	111
David Gahan	113
Alan Charles Wilder	115

Chapter 4 Politics 118
Charles Edward Leatherland 118
Angela Evans Smith - Politician 122

Chapter 5 Our Footballers 125
Michael Kightly 125
Andy Barcham 127
Darren Caskey 128
Stewart Robson 130
Justin Edinburgh 132
Freddy Eastwood 136
Steve Jones 139
Stephen Tilson 140
James Tomkins 142

Chapter 6 Other Sports -persons 145
Eamonn Martin - Athlete 145
Rob Denmark – Athlete 150
Bob Downs - Cyclist 151
Mark Foster - Swimmer 152
Jillean Hipsey - Netball 155
Stuart Bingham - Snooker 160
Terry Marsh - Boxer 164
George Sawyer – Speed Boats 168
Mat Whitlock - Gymnast 171
Perry McCarthy – Formulla 1 173

Chapter 7 That's It 181
Other books by the Author 182
References 187

The Author

Kenneth (Ken) Frederick Porter was born in Laindon in 1944 in the shadow of St Nicholas Church. The family moved to Langdon Hills in 1963 following compulsory purchase by the then Basildon Corporation. He has lived there ever since other than for a five year spell living in Southminster when he first got married to Carol in 1965.

He went to two local schools, first Markham's Chase (now Janet Dukes) and then Laindon High Road School (now demolished for a housing estate). His only real interest at school was sport and history. On leaving school he managed to get a job at Ford Motor Company in Dagenham and his short spell there convinced him that he would have to get a qualification, so after several years of study he qualified as an accountant, retiring as Company Secretary and Finance Director of a small Public Company.

His main passion has been playing and coaching cricket (Advance/Level 3 coach). He has been married to Carol for 50 years and thanks her for all her support throughout the years. They have three children, Craig, married to Debbie and living in Langdon Hills with children Kayleigh, Kyran, and Callum, Kevin married to Angela living in the French Alps with one son Archie and Joanne married to Mathew with daughters Anna and Lucy also living in the French Alps.

Since retiring local history has taken up his time and he is involved in two local history groups – Laindon and District Community Archive and Basildon Borough Heritage. He is also currently church warden at St Nicholas Church, Laindon. He gives talks on the local history of Laindon and Basildon and this is his sixth book the previous five he wrote with colleague Stephen Wynn. There are more in the pipe line.

Acknowledgement and Contributors

Writing a book of this nature requires a considerable amount of research and I could not have completed it without the help and co-operation of a large number of people and interested groups.

My thanks must start with the individuals who have allowed me to write about their careers and reproduce some of their photographs. I would also like to express my appreciation to those who helped me to verify information that I have sourced, members of the Laindon and District Community Archive and the Basildon Borough Heritage Groups, in particular Denise Rowling, Jo Cullen, Sue Ranford and Eric Lamb and a special thank you to Dawn Knox for her help with the cover andto John and Ann Rugg who painstakingly proof read the manuscript.

I must also so thank those that answered many of my face-book requesting either giving or confirming important information. I have made every effort to contact the copyright holders of images and documents in this book. I apologise to anybody not properly acknowledge or whom I have not managed to trace.

Contributors

Paul Sticklands, Eric Lamb, Jean Pattle, John Peters, Nina and Colin Humphrey Perry McCarthy, Eamonn Martin, Graham Bonney, John Georgiadis, Terry Lockhart, Marjorie Hewett, John Georgiadis, Tito G Correa, Joe Bruce, Steve Burton, Milly Baker, George Sawyer and Max Whitlock.

Introduction

Laindon and surrounding district has a long, varied and unique history. However it does not all revolve around castles, stately homes or battles but around people and after several years of researching the history of the district, I have become pleasantly surprised how many people born or lived in the area who have become nationally or internationally known and in many cases made a considerable mark on our society. So it was my initial intention of publishing a book based on Laindon's famous. However, in recent years my research has progressed outside the confines of Laindon and has taken in the whole of the Basildon Borough. In so doing I have come across a considerable number of people who have had a connection with the borough and fall into the above category and therefore must be included so that the people of Basildon are aware of their rich pedigree.

We have many who have made a name for themselves in the sporting and entertainment world but there are many more that fall into the categories of religion, education, politics, business etc.

Whether you are aware of the people I have written about will depend on your personal interests but I believe you will agree that they all had or have an ability, skill or talent that has made them stand out. For example, I have included my sister, because so often I have heard her referred to as a 'living legend' but unless you were interested in netball you may well not have heard of her. Also there maybe the odd name that possibly falls outside the category of famous people but I have included them because of the impact I believe they have made on society. Marion Wilberforce for example, Second World War female pilot.

As I as was writing the book I kept coming across more and more young people from the area that are making their mark so I am very conscious that there are many that I will miss and if there are some obvious ones I apologise for their omission.

To capture your interest I toyed with which category to start with and I probably should have started with either Sport or Entertainment, Joan Sims for example but decided that it seemed sensible to go right back in time to the 17th Century to the time of the emerging religious sect 'The Puritan's'.

Chapter 1 - The Puritans

I believe we have all heard of the Puritans, but who were they. Well they were a group of English Protestants who came to prominence in the late 16th and 17th centuries, culminating in the 1650s under Oliver Cromwell. They worked tirelessly towards religious, moral and social reforms and therefore became particular unhappy with the speed of reformation of the Church of England under Elizabeth 1 and the tolerance the established Church was showing towards the Catholic Church.

They attempted to simplify and regulate forms of worship but were severely restricted by laws controlling the practice of religion. In many cases persecution led to many emigrating permanently or for short periods to the Netherlands. Then in the 1620/40s many started to emigrate to the Americas in particular the new province known as New England, it became known as the 'Great Migration' with the individuals being referred to as 'The Pilgrim Fathers'.

Essex was a hot spot for Puritans so it is not surprising that we have a number of Basildon ancestors who attempted the arduous journey into the virtually unknown. It is worth noting that Elizabeth Cromwell (nee Bourchier) lived at Little Stambridge Hall, Essex and it is possible this is where she met Oliver Cromwell and it is possible he owned the Hall for a time.

The Mayflower – Christopher Martin

I am sure many of you have heard of the Mayflower and Christopher Martin who was the ship's governor who set sail from Plymouth for America with 102 passengers known as the Pilgrim Fathers but also known as Separatists and approximately 30 crew.

Christopher was from Great Burstead, Essex and the first record we find of him is his marriage to Mary Prower a widow who had a son Solomon from her previous marriage to Edward Prower. Christopher and Mary had their own son Nathaniel in 1609.

It is difficult to establish what sort of person Christopher was; he was no doubt a religious person with strong views but at the same time appears to have been mistrusted by many of his compatriots. He was a Merchant by trade but without the required seven year apprenticeship at times caused him problems, for example in 1607 he was sued by another Merchant George Hills, the outcome however is unknown. Though whatever problems he had did not appear to get in his way as he managed to build himself a sizeable estate which included three properties.

In 1611 he was appointed church warden of Great Burstead but at the Easter service in 1612 he caused a stir with Mary refusing to kneel to take Holy Communion. These actions probably were their first sign of their early Puritan views.

By 1620 he was residing in Billericay and having further problems with the church through his son Nathanial and step son Solomon behaviour towards the church. They had refused to participate in the recital of phrases from the Book of Common Prayer during conformation.

By now he had already sold some of his properties with the view of emigrating to America, his first sale being on the 22 June 1617 and his last on 8 June 1620. In January 1616/7 he had paid monies towards the transportation of two people, Ralph Hamer being one to the Colony of Virginia. Obviously his Puritans ideals were gathering pace.

He seemed to have problems regarding financial matters and at one point was reported by a church official for not providing the financial accounts he maintained during the time he was church warden. Similar problems were going to occur when he became governor of first the ship Speedwell and then the Mayflower.

In early 1620 he purchased four shares in the Virginia Company (London) from George Percy for himself and three others, presumably his wife and two sons. As it turned out his son Nathaniel did not sail with them and nothing is known why or what happened to him. His place appears to have been taken by their young servant John Langemore.

He had associated himself with London Merchants known as Merchant Adventurers who were providing financial investment and arranging the emigration and settlement in America with the Leiden (Leyden) congregation of the Netherlands, the congregation being mainly Englishmen who had previously emigrated there.

He was appointed purchasing agent, initially connected to the ship 'Speedwell' sister ship to the Mayflower but this became unseaworthy so he took over the function with regards to the Mayflower. His role along with two others John Carver and Robert Cushman who were based in the Netherlands was to purchase supplies and foodstuffs such as beer, wine, hardtack, salted beef and pork, dried peas, fishing supplies, muskets, armour, clothing, tools, trade goods for Indians, and the screw-jack which would prove to be useful in ship-structure prior to their arrival in America. He purchased most of his supplies in Southampton but is also understood to have also procured food locally and in fact the flour of the voyage was possible milled at one of the two windmills on Bell Hill.

As previously stated he did not endear himself well to the Separatists, however. Robert Cushman, one of the Pilgrim's business leaders, reported:

'Near £700 hath been bestowed at Hampton, upon what I know not, Mr. Martin saith he neither can, nor will give any account of it; and if he be called upon for accounts, he crieth out of unthankfulness for his pains and care, that we are suspicious of him, and flings away, ... he ... so insulteth over our poor people, with such scorn and contempt, as if they were not good enough to wipe his shoes. It would break your heart to see his dealing, and the mourning of our people; they complain to me, and alas! I can do nothing for them. If I speak to him, he flies in my face as mutinous, and saith no complaints shall be heard or received but by himself, and saith they are forward and waspish, discontented people, and I do ill to hear them. There are others that would lose all they have put in, or make satisfaction for what they have had, that they might depart; but he will not hear them, nor suffer them to go ashore, lest they should run away. The sailors are so offended at his ignorant boldness in meddling and controlling in things he knows not what belongs to, as that some threaten to mischief him.'

What action was taken if any is unknown but despite the seriousness of their concerns the Leiden congregation still assigned him to governor of the 'Speedwell'.

It is understood that a meeting of the Pilgrim Fathers was held just prior to their sailing involving at least 35 devout Non-Conformists. The meeting is said to have taken place at the Chantry House, Billericay one of Christopher Martin's properties. The house had been built in 1510 or a major renovation of a previous house going back to the mid- 1300s which had been built for the Chantry Priest of Chantry Chapel St Mary Magdalem. It would have been at this meeting that Christopher and family were able to say their goodbyes. There were two other Billericay men travelling with them, Peter Browne and Richard Britteridge.

Figure 1 Mayflower

The Mayflower had been hired in London and sailed to Southampton in July 1620. The majority of the Pilgrims from Leiden travelled in the Speedwell from Delfshaven, Netherlands to Southampton. The plan was for both ships to sail to Northern Virginia but on Speedwell's journey to Southampton it started leaking, a week was spent patching her up and eventually on 5 August they set sail but she started leaking again so they disembarked at Dartmouth for further repairs. They continued their journey on the 21 August but after sailing approximately 300 miles 'Speedwell' started to leak again so both ships returned to Plymouth.

The following is from Speedwell's log:

Saturday, Aug. 26.   -   About 100 leagues [300 miles] from Land's End. Ship leaking badly. Hove to. Signalled MAY-FLOWER, in company. Consultation between masters, carpenters, and principal passengers. Decided to put back into Plymouth and determine whether pinnace is seaworthy. Put about and laid course for Plymouth.

Frustrated by all the problems they decided to leave Speedwell behind, many quit the voyage and others transferred to the Mayflower along with their cargo causing considerable overcrowding.

Monday, Aug. 28   -   At anchor in Plymouth harbour. Conference of Chief Colonists and officers of May-Flower and Speedwell. No special leak could be found but it was judged to be the general weakness of the ship and that she would not prove sufficient for the voyage. It was resolved to dismiss her the Speedwell and part of the company and proceed with the other ship.

After living on the ships for a month and a half the Mayflower finally left Plymouth on the 6 September 1620. The voyage at first was fairly uneventful the only major problem as one would expect was sea-sickness, however in the latter part of the voyage they encountered a number of storms to the point that it was not safe to use the ships sail's so at times they just drifted. So considering the difficult crossing in a ship that appears to be just about seaworthy and unsanitary conditions, it is surprising that there were only two deaths a crew member and a passenger. There was however some joy with births of two baby boys, Peregrine White to Susanna White and another aptly named Oceanus Hopkins, Peregrine is believed to have died at the age of seven.

The Hudson River was their original destination as they had received good reports on the area back in the Netherlands. On the 9 November after 66 days at sea they spotted land (A spot they would later call Cape Cod). Considering the bad weather they only missed the Hudson River by a few degrees so they decided to head south towards the mouth of the river but further bad weather nearly caused them to shipwreck, so they decided to explore Cape Cod and anchored in what is now Province town Harbour a couple of days later. After a month and a half exploring the area they decided on the 25 December where to build their plantation and Plimouth (Plymouth) came into being.

Figure 2 Mayflower Compact

It would appear that Robert Cushman who had been one of the early organizers of the project and was to be Christopher Martin's assistant did not in the end sail with the Mayflower, possibly due to the fact that he was not very well or frustrated with his relationship with Martin. It was also reported by William Bradford one of the Pilgrims in his journal of Plimouth Plantation

(1646) that somewhere into the voyage the Leidens had had enough of Christopher Martin and chose the more popular John Carver to take over.

On board ship on the 11 November just before disembarking the Separatists decided they needed a governing document which became known as the 'Mayflower Compact', forty one of the adult passengers signed the document including Christopher Martin and the other two Billericay Pilgrims, Peter Browne and Richard Britteridge.

'In the name of God, Amen. We, whose names are underwritten, the loyal subjects of our dread Sovereign Lord King James, by the Grace of God, of Great Britain, France, and Ireland, King, defender of the Faith, etc.

Having undertaken, for the Glory of God, and advancements of the Christian faith and honour of our King and Country, a voyage to plant the first colony in the Northern parts of Virginia, do by these present, solemnly and mutually, in the presence of God, and one another, covenant and combine ourselves together into a civil body politic; for our better ordering, and preservation and furtherance of the ends aforesaid; and by virtue hereof to enact, constitute, and frame, such just and equal laws, ordinances, acts, constitutions, and offices, from time to time, as shall be thought most meet and convenient for the general good of the colony; unto which we promise all due submission and obedience.

In witness whereof we have hereunto subscribed our names at Cape Cod the 11th of November, in the year of the reign of our Sovereign Lord King James, of England, France, and Ireland, the eighteenth, and of Scotland the fifty-fourth, 1620'.

The date 11 November is based on the Julian calendar; the Gregorian calendar was not adopted until 1752 it would have made the date the 21st. Also the 'dread sovereign' referred to in the document used the archaic definition of dread—meaning awe and reverence (for the King), not fear.

What is however very depressing is that within several months of landing almost half the passengers perished in the cold, harsh unfamiliar New England winter. This unfortunately included our Christopher Martin and his family. It would appear that Solomon was the first to die on the 24 December 1620, Christopher died on the 8 January 1621 the day after he had met with John Carver to discuss business and finance. Mary and servant John Langmore also succumbed to the harsh conditions. Richard Britteridge also died, believed to be first to die on board ship after it had cast anchor but Peter Browne appears to have survived although it has been suggested he also died before leaving the ship.

They were all buried in the new Coles Hill Burial Ground. The family is memorialised on the Pilgrim Memorial Tomb, Coles Hill, Plymouth. The three entries for them on the Tomb are "Christopher Martin and his wife", "Solomon Prower" and their servant John Langemore/Langerman named as "John Langmore".

William Bradford also wrote in his Journal that *'Mr Martin, he and all his, dyed in the first infection; not long after the arrival. The death of Christopher Martin removed what might have been a source of future trouble in the life of Plymouth colony'*.

Also, Azel Am, M.D. Member of the Pilgrim Society in his book 'The May-Flower and her Log (1907) with reference to Bradford's journey had this to say:

'From collateral data it appears that he must have been "about forty" years old when he joined the Pilgrims. He appears to have been a staunch "Independent" and to have drawn upon himself the ire of the Archdeacon of Chelmsford. He seems to have been at all times a self-conceited, arrogant, and unsatisfactory man. That he was elected treasurer and ship's "governor" and permitted so much unbridled liberty as appears, is incomprehensible. It was probably fortunate that he died early, as he did, evidently in utter poverty. He had a son, in 1620, apparently quite a grown youth, from which it is fair to infer that the father was at that time "about forty." Of his wife nothing is known. She also died early'.

Bradford goes on to inform us that Martin was appointed the treasurer-agent of the Planter Company, Presumably about the time of the original conclusions between the Adventurers and the Planters, not because he was needed, but to give the English contingent of the Planter body representation in the management, and to allay thereby any suspicion or jealousy. He was, if we are to judge by the evidence in hand concerning his contention and that of his family with the Archdeacon, the strong testimony that Cushman bears against him in his Dartmouth letter of August 17, and the fact that there seems to have been early dissatisfaction with him as "governor" on the ship, a very self-sufficient, somewhat arrogant, and decidedly contentious individual. His selection as treasurer seems to have been very unfortunate, as Bradford indicates that his accounts were in unsatisfactory shape, and that he had no means of his own, while his rather surprising selection for the office of "governor" of the larger ship, after the unpleasant experience with him as treasurer-agent, is difficult to account for, except that he was evidently an active opponent of Cushman, and the latter was just then in disfavour with the colonists. He was evidently a man in the prime of life, an "Independent" who had the courage of his convictions if little discretion, and much of that energy and self-reliance which, properly restrained, are excellent elements for a *colonist.*

The comment he had no means of his own seem a little strange as he at one time owned a considerable estate in the Billericay/Great Burstead area of three properties.

So was Christopher such an unpleasant man or not but whatever, one cannot take it away from him that along with his family and compatriots he was an extremely brave person who wanted to follow his ideals even if it was to the end of the world.

These deaths however did not deter further migrations from Billericay and in 1655 the town of Billerica was established in their honour.

In 1920, at the three-hundredth anniversary of the *Mayflower* sailing, a plaque was unveiled in the United Reform Church in Billericay, Essex, England, to commemorate the Martin family, *Mayflower* emigrants from that town. The plaque names Christopher Martin, Marie Martin, Solomon Prower and John Langerman. Maybe Peter Browne and Richard Britteridge should be added to this plaque. There is also Christopher Martin Road in Basildon.

On the 23 August 1998 Billericay, Essex officially twinned with Billerica in New England. In Billericay there are other historical imagery associated to the Mayflower – Mayflower House, Mayflower Car Services Ltd, Mayflower Hall and Mayflower High School, Mayflower Morris Dancers, Mayflower Retail Park, Mayflower Convalescent Home.

Figure 3 Plaque-United Reform Church - Photograph by Ken Porter

"Next to the fugitives whom Moses led out of Egypt, the little shipload of outcasts who landed at Plymouth are destined to influence the future of the world." *-JAMES RUSSELL LOWELL (American poet from New England)*

Hugh (Hugo) Peters

While waiting for documents to be delivered up from the archives of the Essex Record Office in Chelmsford, I started looking at the various Essex books on the shelves and I came across the following book:- "New light on the Pilgrim story" by the Reverend Thomas W Mason and what a gem I found hidden amongst its pages. A piece of Laindon I was surprised I had not come across before.

Figure 4 Hugo Peters

Many Essex families during the 1600 held strong Puritan beliefs and were supporters of Cromwell and the Parliamentarians. It is therefore not surprising that Essex has a number of famous Puritan ancestors who were to make a considerable contribution to the development of the New World of America.

One such man was Hugh (Hugo) Peters and although he was born in Foy (Fowey), Cornwall he came to preach in Essex after leaving Trinity College, Cambridge with a BA in 1618.

He met a Thomas Hooker a non-conformist (Puritan), at his school in Little Baddow. It is possible that because of his involvement with Hooker, he decided to become a clergyman. He was ordained into the Anglican Church as a Deacon on the 23 December 1621 at Bishop's Palace, London. Just prior to him being ordained he had taken up the post of school master at Laindon and was therefore possibly one of the first teachers to be paid via the Puckles Charity.

The School building and probably where he lived was the timber part of the church of St Nicholas, known as the Priest House. Hugh's salary for teaching in Laindon would have been paid out of the Puckles Charity which had commenced in 1617. John Puckle a local farmer in his will of 1617 gave all his copyhold lands to the church for the maintenance of a schoolmaster to teach the poor of Laindon and Basildon.

Hugh was ordained Priest on the 8th June 1623 again at Bishop's Place, London after obtaining a MA at Trinity College. I assume he had to give up the Laindon teaching post on becoming a Priest and for a short time was Curate at St Nicholas.

He came under the patronage of the Earl of Warwick, and whilst so became curate at Rayleigh, remaining there until 1626. In 1624 he married Elizabeth (nee Cooke) Read(e) the widow of Edmund Read(e) of Wickford. He later became a very popular preacher of St Sepulchre's at Holborn. However he fell out with the church authorities and was imprisoned for six months after leading the congregation at Christ Church in praying for Queen Henrietta Maria (Wife of Charles 1) to give up her Catholicism.

He was released following the Earl of Warwick posting bail. In August 1627 he composed a statement to prove his orthodoxy for the Bishop of London, however later that year he had his licence to preach revoked.

For the next couple of years he travelled back and forth to the Low Lands, serving briefly as the minister at Amelant, an island off Friesland. He also continued to occasionally preach at Rayleigh where the Rector and wardens claimed not to be aware of his suspension to preach. He then had the audacity to preach again at St Sepulchre on behalf of the Queen. On this occasion he was sent to prison for six months without bail.

On his release he became proctor at Friesland University under its rector, William Ames. Staying on the continent he became chaplain to one of the four English regiments in the army of Frederick Henry. Later publishing an account of the army's successes, Digitus Dei (1631).

Then in 1633 he became a pastor at Rotterdam and set out to reform it along Congregationalist lines. In May 1634 William Brereton visited and described Peter as 'a right zealous and worthy man' (Travels in Holland 1644). Brereton was a staunch Puritan; he advocated root and branch reform of the Anglican Church and became a Major General in the Parliamentary Army.

It was not long before pressure was being put on the English Churches in the Netherlands to conform to the doctrines being advocated by Archbishop Laud. So in July 1635 he was off again, deciding to follow many of his Puritan colleagues to America. With his family, which included his step daughter Elizabeth and new husband John Winthrop the younger, he accompanied Sir Henry Vane to New England.

He obviously had an interest in the American colonies because in 1629 he subscribed £50 to the precursor to the Massachusetts Bay Company and attended many of the company meetings for the next year.

He worked tirelessly on behalf of the new colony helping to solve various differences, improving the colonies economy and developing the regions fishery and shipbuilding. He also worked on a programme to readdress seasonal fluctuation of employment of women and children.

In December 1636, Hugh became minister of Salem, Massachusetts, serving on committees to develop a law code for the region. Although he became involved with religious disputes with Sir Henry Vane, he was a popular minister and was actively involved in the civil administration of Salem. He became one of the first governors of Harvard College.

In 1639 following the death of his wife Elizabeth who was several years older than him, he married Deliverance Sheffield. Their only child a daughter was born in October 1640. Then in 1641 he returned to England as one of three agents appointed by the Colony of Massachusetts to drum up new settlers.

However he soon became an active supporter of the Parliament against the King, in the hope of securing a godly reformation of the English church. He became chaplain in the Earl of Essex's army and in the Cromwell's New Model Army.

Although his preaching inspired the soldiers, he still intended to return to America at the end of the First Civil War but Fairfax and Cromwell valued his services so he stayed on and got involved with the struggle between the Army and the Presbyterians (Scots). He accompanied Cromwell on his campaigns during the Second Civil War and was one of the clergymen to support the Army's occupation of London and Pride's Purge, (The purging of members of Parliament hostile to the New Model Army-the purge was led by Colonel Thomas Pride) which led to the trial of King Charles in 1649. He preached during the trial and these sermons were said to have a considerable influence on the outcome of his sentence on the return of King Charles 11.

He stayed active and loyal to Cromwell throughout the period of the Commonwealth. S.R.Gardiner wrote of him: 'it is easy to imagine how he could chat and jest with the soldiers and yet could seize an opportunity to slip in a word on higher matters. His influence must have been such as Cromwell loved-an influence which in every word and action made for concord."

It is reported that he was one of those who worked hard on convincing Cromwell that the King should be brought to Justice. When Charles was arrested he had several conversations with him at Newmarket. Charles is reported to have said: *"that he had often heard talk of him but did not believe he had that solidity in him he found by his discourse"* (A conference betwixt the Kings most Excellent Majesty and Mr Peters, 1647).

He continued to be very active over the next decade only disappearing for short periods from public view due to bouts of illness. In this time he was made a Colonel and became governor of Milford Haven. His last great public act was to preach Oliver Cromwell's funeral sermon in November 1658. He then started to fade from public view mainly because of ill health, other than to declare that the overthrow of Richard Cromwell was 'Very sinful and ruining'.

In August 1660, following the restoration of Charles 11, parliament passed the 'Act of Indemnity and Oblivion' which gave pardon to anybody who had supported the republican (Commonwealth) government of Oliver Cromwell. However Charles retained the right to try for treason those people who had participated in the trial and execution of his father.

Although he had played no direct role in the trial and execution, his reputation and strong association with the commonwealth regime resulted in his arrest with others on charges of treason.

While in prison he was visited by his daughter and wrote possibly his best work, A Dying Fathers Last Legacy to an Only Child (1660).

He along with Sir Henry Vane and eight others were found guilty and sentenced to be Hung, Drawn and Quartered. Hugh was executed on the 16th October 1660 and his head displayed on a pole on London Bridge.

I recalled this story to St Nicholas's first woman priest Reverend Diane Ricketts and when asked a question, I assured her that as a Vicar she would not have been Hung, Drawn and Quartered but instead as a women she would have been burnt at the stake…alive!

In 2013 Tito G Correa while at Homerton College, University of Cambridge submitted his dissertation for the degree of Doctor of Philosophy. His work examined the pre-founding of Harvard College in the seventeenth century Holland, a period referred to as the pre-history of Harvard. The work focused on the efforts of two English Puritan Divines, William Ames (1575-1633) and Hugo Peters (1598-1660).

In his opening gambit on the chapter Peters, he had this to say about him:

'This chapter introduces Hugo Peters, the pragmatic visionary, friend, and admirer of William Ames who became the chief architect of the plan to start a college in the Netherlands and New England. Hugo Peters wore many hats: lecturer, headmaster, minister, entrepreneur, Harvard's overseer, Oliver Cromwell's chaplain and soldier in

the English Civil War. Compared with William Ames, who was an intellectual and prolific writer, Peter was more a man of action, a pragmatist who made things happen. Although he can never be credited with starting a project and seeing it through to culmination because of his involvement in many undertakings, he can, however, be situated in nearly every major event in seventeenth-century Puritanism. His energetic personality was significant in empowering people to take action that projects such as the dream of a college in New England might have taken far longer to reach fruition without his involvement. Regarding the founding of Harvard, for example, it is important to remember that Peter arrived in New England in October 1635 and that, by May of the following year, he had already made arrangements for a college in Salem and had presented an official proposal outlining the project etc, etc.'

It's amazing how many talented man of this era ended up being executed

There is a twist to this story so read on..........

Reade family of Wickford

Elizabeth Winthrop (nee Reade)

The twist-Just prior to Hugo Peters taking his family to the New World is that his stepdaughter, Elizabeth, was married in July of the same year to John Winthrop the younger and they sailed soon afterwards in the ship 'Abigail' to Massachusetts. John's father also John was already in Massachusetts, he had led a group of Puritans to the New World in 1629. John the Younger had followed his father to Massachusetts in 1631 but had come back two years later before returning with Elizabeth, his second wife with who he had eight children with.

Both Johns became influential people holding governorships etc. in the New World. Wickford Rhode Island, takes its name from Elizabeth birthplace.

In a letter from her grandson John Winthrop (son of Major General Waitstill Winthrop) in 1704 he states *"Wickford also had its name from her being ye place of Her Nativity in old England."*

There is also a spring on the outskirts of East Greenwich, Rhode Island, that was named Elizabeth Spring's after her by Roger Williams. The spring was first used by the Indians who travelled the Pequot trail and it is believed that Elizabeth probably stopped to drink at the spring on her way to New London from Boston.

In 1866 a millstone with a marble tablet bearing the following

Figure 5 Shop in Wickford-Rhode Island

inscription was placed by the spring by Dr. James Etherdge:

'Elizabeth Spring's, so called from Mistress Elizabeth Winthrop drinking at it in her travels up to Connecticut in ye beginning of ye country as early as 1645. Roger Williams laments; ' Here is the spring, say I, with a sigh, but where is Elizabeth? My charity answers: She is gone to the Eternal Spring and Fountain of Living Waters' (Source article: 'Elizabeth Spring – A Mirror of History by Marion Fry).

Our Elizabeth must have been a powerful women in her own right but her story does not end here, her descendants just happen to be John Kerry (Currently United States Secretary of State) and Ex-Presidents George H W Bush and W Bush.

Surely it is time that Wickford, England erect a memorial in the town to Elizabeth and twin with Wickford Rhode Island.

Elizabeth died on 14 November 1672 in Hartford, Connecticut, United

Figure 6 Wickford - Rhode Island

States. John the Younger died on 6 April 1676 In Boston, Connecticut, United States.

Edmund Reade (Colonel) was baptised in Wickford on the 23 May 1563 and married Elizabeth (nee Cooke) at Pebmarsh, Essex in 1594 following the death of his first wife Thomasin Wallenger who died in Wickford in 1592. Edmund held a considerable amount of land in the Wickford area and his ancestry can be traced back in the area of Wickford and Runwell to at least the late 1400's. Although of minor gentry he was obviously a fairly wealthy man and this is borne out by his will of 1623.

The will showed he was a fairly generous man, for example he gave twenty shillings to the poor of Wickford, five pounds to his servant John Weald and two shillings to his other servants. Most of his lands etc went to his eldest son William but he made sure that the rest of his children were well catered for. He died on the 1 December 1623 aged 60 and is buried in Wickford.

Elizabeth Winthrop was not his only daughter that emigrated to America. Margaret Lake (nee Reade) and her two daughters, Hannah and Martha along with their brother Thomas all appeared to have sailed on 'Abigail' to Massachusetts.

For some unexplained reason Margaret had left her husband John Lake and remaining children in England. John Lake had been born on 26 September 1590 in Norman-town, Yorkshire and following the death of his father (also John) in 1612 he inherited Great Fanton Hall, North Benfleet, he married Margaret in 1616 at North Benfleet.

Why did Margaret who was only in her early thirties leave behind her husband and some of her children. It has been suggested considering the family were wealthy Landowners, owning land not only in North Benfleet but also in neighbouring parishes of Nevendon, Basildon, Wickford and Rawreth that she looked to the colonies of North America for sanctuary of her religious beliefs. Or another possibility was that she had lost at least two of her children to the plague, or was it an unhappy marriage?

One must be aware of the religious upheaval and civil unrest that the country was going through at the time. The populous were unhappy with James 1 and later Charles 1 which eventually ended in two Civil Wars. This unrest was as evident in Essex as anywhere in the country and preceding the Civil Wars saw approximately 30,000 people leave our shores for new lives in New England in what has been referred to as the Great Migration. This migration had begun in 1630 when Elizabeth Winthrop's father-in-law John Winthrop Sr. with a small fleet of Puritan settlers founded Massachusetts Bay Colony, albeit Christopher Martin had sailed some ten years

Figure 7 Great Fanton Hall. Basildon Heritage collection

earlier to North America.

Margaret (Reade) was born on 11 July 1598 in North Benfleet. The daughters that went with her were Hannah who was according to the North Benfleet's All Saints Church born/baptised on 3 July 1621 and Martha was born/baptised 20 July 1624. An interesting side piece is that their grandfather John Lake Snr, served as juror for Barstable Hundred in the year of the Armada 1588.

As you would expect the land these settlers occupied was the tribal homeland of native Indians. Where Margaret and daughters landed was the homeland of the Wampanoag Indians. By 1637 the Massachusetts Bay Colony had conquered the various tribes in particular the Pequot Indians and to bring the land under control gave to John Winthrop Jr some land. Some eight years later John visited the area to finalise his plans and his sister in law Margaret Lake (nee Reade) joined him and was to be the first woman to set foot in the area that later become known as New London.

Whatever Margaret's reason for leaving England, she still tried to keep in touch with her husband. Her step-father, Rev. Hugh Peters, wrote from London to John Winthrop Jr. in 1654 to say that "John Lake is alive and lusty". He wrote again in 1657 saying: "John Lake lives still" however he died some four years later.

Margaret's daughter, Hannah at the age of twenty-two in 1643 married John Gallop and she became part of a famous frontier family. John Gallop fought in many of the frontier wars and Hannah's sons, John and William followed in his footsteps and her grandsons, great-grandsons and great-great-grandsons continued in the tradition that would see them fight in the War of Independence and the American Civil War. Hannah died a wealthy and respected women on the 19 December 1675 whose descendants like Elizabeth Winthrop include Presidents George H.W. and George W Bush.

Margaret had died only three years earlier on the 24 September 1672, in Ipswich, Massachusetts where she had been living at the time with daughter Martha who had married Thomas Harris in 1647. Martha died on the 5 April 1700, in Ipswich, Essex. New England.

Elizabeth, Margaret, Hannah, Martha are just four of the Essex women who had the courage to seek a new life in America and helped to open up its frontiers and they were one of ours.

What happen to Elizabeth and Margaret's brother who had sailed out with them, well at some later date he returned to England and became a Colonel in Oliver Cromwell's army; General Monck following the siege of

Stirling Castle in August 1651 left Thomas in command. Then following the death of Cromwell, Thomas assisted General Monck in the restoration of Charles 11.

What a family but we must move on.

Chapter 2 - Various

John Pell..Priest

Figure 8 John Pell

John Pell was born on 1 March 1911 at Southwick, Sussex, he was the second of two sons of John Pell and Mary (nee Holland) and it is reported that they came from ancient Lincoln stock. Pell's father died in 1616 and left him an excellent library, his early education was at a newly founded free school at Steyning, Sussex. At the age of thirteen he went to Trinity College, Cambridge. He was fluent in Latin, Greek and Hebrew and graduated with a BA in 1628 and MA in 1630. In 1631 he was incorporated in the University of Oxford. Pell was a striking figure, remarkably handsome, with dark hair and eyes. He was strong, with excellent posture and a good voice. He married Ithumaria Reginolles on the 3rd July 1632 and they were to have four sons and four daughters. Ithumaria died young on the 11 September 1661 and Pell remarried sometime before 1669.

During the early years of his marriage he added, Arabic, Italian, Spanish, French and Low and High Dutch (German) to his vocabulary and was becoming well known for his knowledge of not only languages but also of mathematics.

Between 1630 and 1638 he was assistant master at Collyer's School in Horsham and teacher at Samuel Hartlib's short lived Chichester Academy in Sussex, presumably teaching languages or mathematics.

In 1638 a Theodore Haake persuaded him to move to London and teach Mathematics. Although, as a mathematician he soon achieved a considerable reputation, he was not a forceful person and throughout his life he needed friends to push him forward and recommend him to men of influence.

While in London, Haake recommended him to the Lord Bishop of Lincoln who requested Pell to dine with him. The Bishop was obviously impressed with him and offered him a Benefice. Pell thanked his Lordship but turned it down as he had decided to make mathematics his main career. The Bishop accepted his point of view but requested that they became friends and that he would visit as often as possible. Pell never did.

Haake then heard that Martin Hortensius, the professor of mathematics at Amsterdam had died. He immediately contacted Sir William Boswell, Charles 1 ambassador in Holland and in December 1643, Pell became Hortensius' successor. Then in June 1646 he was invited by the Prince of Orange to become professor of philosophy and mathematics at Breda in the newly founded academy with an annual salary of 1000 guilders. The Dutch were jealous of this foreigner and his duties were restricted to those of professor of mathematics.

Then with the First English-Dutch War imminent, Pell return to London in 1652 and Cromwell's government gave him an annual salary of £200 as 'Professor of Mathematics', but there is no evidence of any teaching. Two years later in 1654 again on Haake's recommendation, Cromwell sent him to Switzerland on a diplomatic mission at an increased salary of £600. His mission was to try and persuade the protestant cantons of France to join a continental protestant league headed by England.

He returned to England just before Oliver Cromwell's death but was unable to see him. During his absence, Haake had taken care of his financial and family affairs.

Following the death of Oliver Cromwell in 1658, Richard, his son, succeeded him as Protector. It would appear that Pell did not receive all his pay for working in Europe, so on the return of Charles II in May 1660, Dr Sanderson, Bishop of Lincoln persuaded Pell to take Holy orders.

He was ordained deacon and priest in 1661 and in the same year the King gave him the living of Fobbing, Essex. Two years later in 1663 the Lord Bishop of London, Gilbert Sheldon, also gave him the living of Laindon – cum – Basildon. Both posts he was to hold until his death.

Our parish, during this period, had become known as the "Scurvy Parsonage of Lanedon-cum-Basseldon", because along with neighbouring parishes they had become infamous for being extremely unhealthy areas.

Mr Edward Waller on the death of the Countess of Warwick wrote:
"Curst be already those Essexian plaines where….Death and horrour reignes---etc"

It is recorded that seven curates died at Fobbing during

Figure 9 St Nicholas Church, Laindon. By king permission of Bob Fisher

Pell's first ten years and in sixteen years six that had been his curates at Laindon had died. It also appears that his wife, servants and grandchildren succumbed to the unhealthy surroundings.

On Gilbert Sheldon being made Archbishop of Canterbury in 1663 he appointed Pell to be one of his domestic chaplains. On one occasion when the opportunity arose Pell complained to the archbishop at Lambeth of the unhealthiness of his benefice, the archbishop's reply was – 'I do not intend that you should live there' 'No' replied Pell, 'but your Grace does intend that I shall die there'.

"Kill-priest" was another name also given to the parish. "The Scurvy Parsonage" is the title given to the small book on the history of the St Nicholas church written by Colin Alderman in 1985 during the Reverend Nihal Paul incumbency.

How different it was going to be 250 years later when people were eager to leave the confines of London for the fresh air and healthy environment of Laindon.

Pell took the degree of D.D. (Doctor of Divinity) in 1663 and in the same year he became one of the first fellows of the Royal Society of London. Christopher Wren, 1663 and Isaac Newton, 1672 are two other famous names who were elected 'Fellows of the Royal Society'. Around this time he became responsible for the reconstruction of the Prayer Book Kalendar assisted by Sancroft who later became Archbishop of Canterbury.

In 1664 the Royal Society formed several committees and Dr Pell found himself a member of those in charge of Mechanical and Optical inventions as well as being responsible for reporting and conducting experiments on natural phenomena. Later he was added to the committee on agriculture. He was elected to the council in 1675 and the following year made a Vice-President.

In 1681 he reported at a meeting that he had translated most of Lazarus Erckers famous book on minerals *'Beschrecbung allerfurnemstenmineralischen Ertzt (1574)'*, into English. This was just one of his many publications; his first mathematical publication was *'An idea of Mathematics'*. A publication to simplify the study of mathematics, there were to be many more publications, either in English, Latin or both.

George Goring the Earl of Norwich, in 1647 sent his grandson Lord Brereton to Breda to receive tuition from Dr. Pell. He became a good practitioner, especially in algebra. It is said that never was there a greater love between master and scholar, than between Dr Pell and Lord Brereton, who was to come to his aid in 1665 when the plague forced him to leave London. At the time he had been boarding in a house owned by a John Collins. He now moved into Brereton Hall in Cheshire and stayed there until Lord Brereton's death in

March 1680.

Dr Pell then moved into obscure lodgings, three storeys high, in Jermyn Street, London, next to Ship Inn and it was in 1680 that he was imprisoned for debt.

Although it appears he was a riotous, enthusiastic and skilful preacher he did not spend much time in his parishes, he left them in the capable hands of his curates. The problem being was by the time he had paid them there was very little left. In fact he became so insolvent that, he actually had two periods of imprisonment.

Anthony Wood wrote in his diary:

' He was a shiftless man as to worldly affairs and his tenants and relations dealt so unkindly to him that they cozened him of the profits of his parsonage and kept him so indigent, that he wanted necessaries, even ink and paper, to his dying day'.

After his spell in prison, Dr. Daniel Whistler provided the now totally impoverished mathematician accommodation at the College of Physicians. They enjoyed each other's company, eating and drinking too much, which unfortunately affected Dr. Pell's health and because of this he was forced to move in with one of his grandchildren in St Margaret's churchyard, Westminster, near the tower in June 1683. He later transferred to lodgings of a Mr Cothorne in Dyot Street, Westminster. Cothorne who was a reader in St Giles-in-the-Fields.

Dr Pell died there on Saturday 12th December 1685 and was buried by the charity of Dr. Richard Busby, schoolmaster at Westminster and Dr. Sharp, Dean of Norwich and rector of St Giles-in-the-Fields. His body was laid in a vault belonging to the rector at a cost of £10.

He could not be persuaded to make a will, so his books, papers etc, went to his son-in-law, Captain Raven who sold them to Dr Richard Busby. Dr. Pell had a brother, a surgeon and practitioner in physics, who had purchased an estate from the natives of New York and when he died he left it to his nephew John Pell who was a justice of the peace in New York and son of Dr. Pell.

Considering his reputation as a mathematician, based on his impressive knowledge of mathematical literature, his devotion to algebra and being the first inventor of that excellent method of marginal working in algebra, it seems incredible that he died penniless and of a broken heart.

Dr. John Pell believed it was with God's help that he was able to solve so many of the questions.

Oh! By the way he invented the mathematical division sign.

Some years ago, I visited the church in the hope of finding his grave, only to establish that a new church had been built in the grounds between 1730-34. However to my surprise the burial registers were still in the church and the church warden kindly showed me the entry of John Pell and allowed me to take a photograph of the entry.

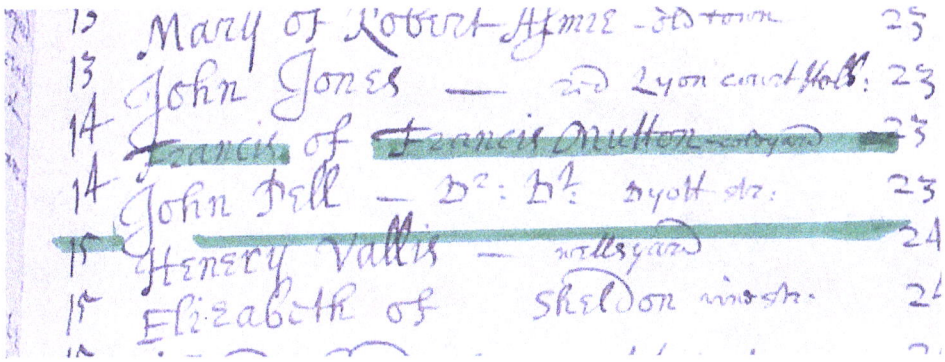

Figure 10 John Pell's death entry in the Church register-Photograph by Ken Porter

It is time for us to move into the nineteenth and twentieth Century, the century that was going to bring the district an amazing number of national and international individuals from various walks of life.

Nathaniel Woodard....................Educationalist

So we now jump forward a hundred and twenty five years to whom I believe is one of Basildon's most remarkable persons, although today not many local people seemed to know of him.

Puckles Charity School based at St Nicholas church had been educating the poor of Laindon and Basildon since the early 1620s until 1877. Private schools around the country were looking after the wealthy but who was looking after the education of the middle sector of society?

This was the concern of Nathaniel Woodard who was born on the 21st March 1811 (St Benedict's Day). 'Labour and obedience' is the motto of Benedictines. It was going to be this motto that helped drive Nathaniel to succeed in establishing a form of education to rival that of the State.

This what Sir John Otter on Nathaniel's life published in 1925 had to say in his opening two paragraphs: '*In the middle of the last century Nathaniel Woodard conceived a magnificent scheme for uplifting of the Church and nation by providing a system of education by means of cheap boarding schools for sons of persons of moderate, or less than moderate, pecuniary means.*

Figure 11 Priest House, St Nicholas Church, Laindon. Ken Porter's collection

The state of middle-class education was at the time, as everyone knows, lamentable. The education of the poor had become, in some degree, a matter of national concern: our public schools invited the wealthy; but the children of the classes in an intermediate state were dependent on private enterprise and often became an open prey to bad influences.'

His father was a country gentleman of a small estate, living at the time at Basildon Hall also referred to as Barstable Hall. The Hall was demolished in October 1961 to make way for new housing in the East Thorpe and Crickett Hill area not far away from the Basildon New Town Centre. It must not be confused with Basildon Cottage that was situated at the end of Hotwater lane.

Nathaniel was the ninth of twelve children, so although his father was living the life of a gentleman, the family were relatively poor and it was this that obviously drove him in later life.

He did not go to school even though Puckles Charity School was only a mile or so away. His mother was a deeply religious women and his religious sense, deep and exacting from very early years, was strengthened and directed by her example and teaching. Therefore from an early age Nathaniel believed that his vocation in life was to take Holy Orders.

We are aware that his mother took him to Laindon Church. However we are not sure whether this was St Nicholas Church, Laindon or Holy Cross, Basildon. With reference to Laindon, we would assume St Nicholas but we have to remember that the Priest's living up to the 1970's was Laindon-cum-Basildon and Holy Cross was initially a chapel to St Nicholas.

Figure 12 Nathaniel Woodard

To obtain Holy orders you had to graduate from Oxford or Cambridge but his father could not afford to send him there. He did instead send him to read with Rev. W Stratton, Rector of Boughton, Norfolk where he followed a course of study.

Sometime in early 1833 his fortune changed as he received sufficient funds for a University Career (believed to be from two aunts). He chose Oxford but it was about this time that he also became engaged to be married to Elizabeth Harriet Brill of an Essex family.

He entered Magdalen Hall in July 1834. Married Elizabeth at Netteswell, Essex on the 24th March 1836 and with this change in his family life he found it difficult to study and it was not until 1840 that he took his degree.

He was eventually ordained on 6th June 1841 by the Bishop of London, Charles James Blomfield.

In his first curacy at St Bartholomew's, Bethnal Green he started a school for children of deprived parishioners. He then moved onto St James the Greater, Clapton, however he fell out over a sermon he gave with Bishop of London and with the help of friends managed to obtained curacy at St Mary de Haura Church, New Shoreham, in 1846

He immediately opened up a day school in his vicarage and in 1848 he started up St Nicholas School where he took in Boarders. This school eventually became the present day Lancing College. Nathaniel believed and wrote in 1849

Figure 13 Basildon Hall. Basildon Heritage collection

that the poor could not be successfully educated or benefited unless the middle classes were educated. So he set himself the task to provide a good and complete education for the middle classes, where pupils were to be taught the fear and honour of God according to the doctrines of the Catholic Faith as set out in the Prayer Book of the Church of England.

He became ill in 1848 but this gave him time to write and publish, *'A plea for the middle classes'* calling of the need to provide a good and complete education for the middle class at a fee that most could afford. Although he accepted day schools, he preferred boarding schools because he wanted to keep the influences of home from them

It was from these beginnings that he started to work full time in promoting educational projects, resigning his curacy in 1850 to concentrate on fund raising he appeared to have the charisma to attract a number of sponsors.

The Saturday Review in 1853 had this to say about him:*'Mr Woodard is and is not, a remarkable man. He is uncompromising, stiff and resolute – some people might say obstinate. He is a man of one idea but he pursues that one idea with unflagging energy and considerable savoir faire.'*

Figure 14 Lancing College

Initially he ignored female education but in 1855 he helped a girl's school in Sussex and in 1874 his first girls school St Anne's School at Abbots Bromley was founded.

In 1870 Oxford University awarded him the degree of DCL and he was made Canon of Manchester Cathedral by Gladstone which carried a stipend of £2,000 a year.

He went on to establish 11 schools in his life time and the Woodard Corporation now controls the largest group of independent Church Of England Schools in England and Wales. Today there are 46 schools under the influence of the Woodard Corporation (Primary and Secondary).

Nathaniel died on the 25th April 1891 and his tomb is in the Chapel of Lancing College.

At the beginning of annual Chapter meetings of the Woodard

Corporation the following words are read: 'Nathaniel Woodard, Clerk in Holy Orders, sometime Canon of Manchester, who was called to rest on the 25th day of April 1891 and whose body lies buried at Lancing College, founded this Corporation in the faith and fear of Almighty God, for the love of his Church and the good of his country.'

On the 24th November 2011 at Westminster Abbey a National Service of Thanksgiving was held to celebrate the 200 years anniversary of his birth.

Would it not be fitting for the Basildon Council to honour one of its greatest sons with a plaque in the town centre?

Dr Henry Selby Hele-Shaw the Billericay man who gave Churchill's "Heroes" a boost.

The 19th Century saw much advancement in many fields progress, typically the Railways Electricity and in Automobiles. Such names as Michael Faraday, Isambard Kingdom Brunel, Robert Stephenson George Stephenson, Sir Joseph Whitworth are well known. The name Henry Selby Hele – Shaw is not so well known, although subsequent development of one of his many inventions had a great significance for British aircraft during World War 2. Some of the inventors who created these advances in technology were practical men whereas others were academics. Henry Selby Hele – Shaw excelled in both aspects.

Figure 15 Dr Henry Selby Hele-Shaw

Dr Hele-Shaw was born in the year 1854 in Billericay where he lived for some seven years. Then throughout his life he moved around the UK, living in the Isle of Man, Bristol, Liverpool and Ross-on-Wye where he died in 1941 aged 86.

In 1861 along with his father Henry, a successful solicitor, mother Marion and two younger brothers he moved to the Isle of Man, his mother and father had a large family of thirteen children. Some eleven years later 1872 he became apprenticed to

Edwin Roach of the Roach and Leaker's Mardyke Iron works in the City of Bristol. He was apprenticed as a Millwright and Mechanical Engineer. This set his future career path.

He gained a degree in Mechanical Engineering from University College Bristol in 1880 and was appointed lecturer in Mathematics and Engineering at the College and a year later, aged 27 he became the first Professor of Engineering at the University College. His advance in the academic sphere continued and in 1885 he became the first person to occupy the Chair of Engineering at the University College of Liverpool. Academically he won several Whitworth prizes. He later formed the Whitworth Society which encourages young engineers.

Whilst he was a brilliant Engineer he also had a normal lifestyle he was a member of Clifton Rugby Club (1872 – 73) whilst he lived in Bristol. However there is no record of any of the games that he played.

In the late 1890's, trials for Commercial Motor vehicles took place in Liverpool and Hele-Shaw participated in these events as a judge. His interests in Automobiles lead him to become a founder member of the R.A.C.

At about this time he invented a friction clutch which was fitted to many commercial vehicles of the period.

In 1904 he accepted an invitation to set up a College of Engineering at the Transvaal Technical Institute, of which he became Principal.

In 1909 he became President of the Institute of Automobile Engineers and that of the Institute of Mechanical Engineers in 1922. He also became a Fellow of the Royal Society.

In 1924 Dr Henry Selby Hele-Shaw and T E Beacham patented the design of a hydraulically operated Variable Pitch Propeller "(V.P.P.)" This type of propeller enabled an engine to operate in its economical range of rotational speeds. This concept had been previously displayed in 1921 at the Paris Air Show by a French aircraft firm.

Hele-Shaw's propeller design could be applied to both aircraft and boats. Furthermore its application to aircraft was demonstrated by a development in conjunction with the Gloster Aircraft Company. The Gloster, Hele-Shaw, Beacham Variable Pitch Propeller was adapted and installed and demonstrated on the Gloster "Grebe" aeroplane.

However the design was bulky and heavy thereby limiting its general use in aircraft. Others worked on further developing the concept, namely the Hamilton Standard division of United Aircraft Company and Curtis Wright in the USA developed an electrically controlled variable pitch propeller. The first practical design was demonstrated in 1932.

By this time the aircraft industry in the UK was working on new aeroplane designs and improved engine and propulsion designs were required. Rolls Royce was developing engine types that lead to the famous Merlin and Griffon engines. Another UK Company the de Havilland aircraft (DH) company bought up the UK rights to the American design from Hamilton Standard. Another UK company, Rotol was formed to pursue its own designs of variable pitch propeller.

In 1939 war broke out between Britain and Germany and by mid-1940 the Germans had over-run most of Western Europe and the Luftwaffe were bombing Southern England. The main German fighter was the Messerschmitt 109 (Bf 109) which some felt had a slight edge on both of the RAF's new fighters, the Spitfire and the Hurricane.

In early June 1940 an RAF Engineering officer "Short circuited" official procedures and arranged for one Spitfire aircraft to be fitted with the de Havilland Variable Pitch propeller instead of the standard DH two pitch propeller. DH reacted swiftly and one Spitfire of number 65 squadron was modified to have a VPP. This resulted in an improved performance in the maximum ceiling for the aircraft and its manoeuvrability; it also reduced the length required for take-off and the rate of climb.

When the Under Secretary for Air heard of this news he requested that de Havilland apply this change retrospectively to all Spitfires and Hurricanes. Thus Henry Selby Hele-Shaw's invention in 1924 had evolved into a practical design which improved the performance of the RAF's main fighter aircraft which were used to defeat the Luftwaffe in the Battle of Britain.

After the end of the Battle Churchill famously said - Never was so much owed by so many to so few" should this have included Henry Selby – Shaw?

Henry Selby Hele-Shaw himself retired to Ross on Wye where he died on 30 January 1941 at the age of 86.

As an engineer he embraced a very wide range of interests, he was a co-founder of Vitaulic, which is now a global firm that produces a specialised range of pipe joints and couplings used by many industries, such as oil and gas. He also co-operated with a German Friederich Gall in the design of an armoured diving suit. He also co-operated with many others on designs.

1941 Obituary: "Dr. H.S.Hele-Shaw on January 30th at the age of eighty-six closes a long career spent in furthering the education of engineers, in scientific research work and in the development of numerous inventions. Dr.

Hele-Shaw was widely known in engineering circles throughout the country. The news of his death will be received with sincere sorrow."

Hele-Shaw married Ella Marion Greg Rathbone in 1890 and they had a son and a daughter in July 1916. The Greg Rathbone family were a well-known merchant family in Liverpool. .

Their son Lt Henry Rathbone Hele-Shaw of 70 Squadron RAF was killed on the 19th July 1916 whilst flying a biplane during the Battle of the Somme. He and his observer were killed.

It appears that Henry was identified and buried by the Germans in the village of Le Verguier near St. Quentin where his grave was discovered by advancing British troops in April 1917. Post war he was re-interred at Jeancourt Communal Cemetery, near Peronne.

Edgar Longstaffe..Artist

Figure 16 Grave of Edgar Longstaffe and his wife. St Nicholas Church, Laindon - Ken Porter's photograph.

Edgar was born in 1852, Hammersmith, London. The 1881 census has him born in Derby but the others in London. This just proves how careful you must be when checking digital internet records. His father Edgar Henry Longstaffe was a doctor and a member of the Royal College of Surgeons. His mother Cornelia, nee Buchanan was born in Calcutta, India. Edgar was the youngest of their three children.

He married Clara Mead in 1880, moving first to Newport, Essex then to Liphook, Hampshire, then sometime in the late 1890's they moved to 'Hill View', Basildon Rise, Laindon. Basildon Rise was an unmade road opposite Church Road running up by the side of Laindon Park Junior School. It was part of the Laindon Hall estate. Today it is just a pathway through the wooded area that surrounds the school and is being looked after by a Sunday morning preservation group. There were about nine houses in the Rise and if you take a walk along the path today you will still see signs of where the houses and gardens were and you must be careful of the wells.

Joe Bruce, an old Laindon resident, remembers with affection his first ten years of married life in Basildon Rise. During the 1950's and early 60's. He moved into a bungalow 'Renfern' only a few doors away from 'High View'. The bungalows were all of wooden structure, there was no main drainage, it was an old bucket and bury it job so the gardens must have been very fertile. No wonder the vegetables and orchards flourished in those days. Electricity, gas and water were all laid on. Although when Edgar moved to 'Hill View' it would have been candles, wells, water butts or stand pipes.

Edgar became a prolific painter in oils in vermilion, of landscapes and woodland scenes. He was especially fond of portraying Highland scenery with cattle and excelled in painting of water. Red was a favourite colour of his. He also had a very detailed technique of painting trees using a particularly rich green palette and for this reason his works are instantly recognisable.

His works are often seen in sale rooms although his name is not that well known because he tended to sign his works with either a monogram in red or his initials 'E.L'.

Figure 17 Highland Scene. Ken Porter's collection

The following works were exhibited five times at the Royal Academy, London:-
- Autumn Leaves: Dudley Wood, Essex (1885)
- Felled trees-the month of March: Greenbank, Liphook, Hants. (1886)
- Wagners's Wells: Bramshott, Hants. (1888)
- Winter fuel (1889)
- In Takeley forest-a November day. (1889)
- Wagner's Well, near Liphook, Hants. (1889)

Autumn Leaves, Dudley Wood was also exhibited at the Royal Hibernian Academy, Dublin and was for sale at £5.5 shillings. Today his paintings vary in value from approximately £250 to £2000. One of his most expensive was 'Across the loch' painted in 1891 and sold in 2001 for £1880. He also exhibited at the Birmingham Royal Academy.

To supplement his income he worked for a time during the early 1900's for postcard manufacturers S. Hildesheimer & Co Ltd and Raphael Tuck and Sons. Raphael used to send him to all the principal beauty spots of the British Isles to obtain sketches for reproduction work and a great number of his postcard works are of the Scottish Highlands, with cattle and water. There were the early days of art picture postcards.

Both Edgar and his wife were very enthusiastic church workers under Reverend H. Carpenter, with Edgar becoming Church Warden of St Nicholas, Laindon. Edgar was also a Trustee of the John Puckles' Educational Charity and was signatory to the sale of Puckles farm in 1899 for £900. The 1911 census has the family living at Hill Farm, just east of the Church.

Following the death of his wife in 1922, Edgar's health slowly declined and he died on the 7th December 1933, leaving behind a married daughter, Violet, a son Ernest who was a well-known composer and producer and one grandson. Reverend M. N. Lake officiated and he was buried with his beloved wife, in the churchyard behind the Chancel of St Nicholas Church.

His grave and the Church is part of the Basildon Heritage Trail.

Cecil Alex Hewett ....Archaeologist

The dating of timber-framed buildings was revolutionised from the early 1960s by Cecil Hewett – Cecil died on the 23rd July 1998, and this opening sentence is from his obituary by A Gibson and D Andrews.

Cecil was born in Laindon, Essex on the 26th September 1926 to Alexander and Ivy; they lived in a bungalow call Besancourt in Gloucester Road. The road was situated in the area behind the current Laindon Shopping centre. It was an unmade road and the bungalow today would be described as one of the many plotland buildings in the area. Basic facilities would have been minimal. The bungalow was compulsory purchased and eventually demolished to make way for new housing developments that were engulfing the new Basildon district. Laindon being one of the ancient parishes in the district of Basildon.

He went to Markham's Chase Primary School (now Janet Duke), then to Laindon High Road Secondary School before gaining a scholarship to go to Chelmsford Art College.

Figure 18 Cecil Hewett. By kind permission of Pat Hewett

He was not the sporting type but an artistic flair showed from a young age and he was regarded as an art prodigy. In fact by the time he was eight years old he was very competent with sharp edge carpentry tools and was making superb models of wooden farm machinery. His attention turned from farm buildings to church buildings and by the time he was twelve he was convinced that conventional dating of timber–framed buildings was largely wrong. It was this early appreciation of timber-framed buildings and experience of acquiring knowledge first-hand that set the pattern for his later research. His initial interest obviously came from his father who was a woodworker by trade and by walking and cycling around Essex from his childhood home at Laindon.

His inspiration also possibly came from the massive timber-framed Bell Tower of St Nicholas Church, Laindon, where he was a choir boy, along with his brother Denys and sister Iris. (In the St Nicholas Church are two hymn sheets that were used by Iris...her name appears on both of them).

He was the first one to point out that this church belfry was in fact a Bell Tower, one of a very few in Essex. He built a five foot model of the Tower and it is currently in storage at the Science Museum storage depot at Swindon. (Possibly the most famous world-wide Bell Tower is the Leaning Tower of Pisa, Italy which was erected in 1174).

Figure 19 St Nicholas Church Bell Tower - Photograph by Ken Porter

Basildon though is fortunate to have three Church Bell Towers, one at Ramsden Bell House and the other being the Glass and Steel Bell Tower, situated in front of St Martin's in the Town Centre which was built in 1999 as part of a Millennium project on the initiative of Reverend Lionel Webber, Rector of Laindon-cum-Basildon and Rural Dean of Basildon. It is believed to be the only glass steel tower in the World.

After leaving college he began his working life as a designer in an advertising office. In 1944 he was called up to do his National Service and one of the tests he had to take was to reassemble a Yale lock, he was the only one of his group who achieved the task. He was shipped off to Egypt where he spent the next four years. On returning home he went back to Chelmsford School of Art and then onto the University College, Swansea, qualifying five years later as a silversmith. He then took up teaching his artistic skills in nine Essex schools for the next nineteen years.

Although he was not a motor fanatic he did drive an Armstrong Siddeley Sapphire around Laindon and servicing of the car was taken care of by Parkinson's, a well-known local character, who had a garage in Laindon High Road on the corner of Somerset Road.

He married Marjorie May (Pat) Burge in Brentwood Registry on the 5th

January 1957. Pat at the time was living in Billericay and working in Upminster as a nursery nurse. She met Cecil as she got off the bus just outside Ye Olde Chantry House in Billericay High Street and yes what was Cecil doing, none other than studying the sixteenth century building. When they got married they first lived in Billericay later moving to Coggleshall before settling down in Kelvedon in 1972. He made many of the pieces of furniture for the home in Kelvedon. (Tables, sideboards etc:) His two boys, Cecil and Richard were born in 1956 and 1958 respectively.

Teaching was not really the job he wanted to do but it did allow him spare time to do his own private research and eventually it was this interest in carpentry and the dating of old wooden buildings that eventually changed his life. He started to write and publish articles on carpentry from his own observations, from this he was invited to give lectures at various locations including the Institute of Archaeology in London.

He obviously impressed many people with his enthusiasm and knowledge because following one of these lectures he was approached by the Greater London Council and he found himself in 1972 accepting a position with the Greater London Council Historic Building Division. His reputation was growing and by the time he moved to the Essex Council's Historic Building and Conservation Section at Chelmsford in 1974 as senior officer he had written three books: Development of Carpentry, English Cathedral Carpentry and Church Carpentry.

Considering his humble background his knowledge and artistic skills were considerable. If it was made out of wood he investigated it and wrote about it (timber buildings, farm equipment, doors, windows, and posts etc.) Also because of his artistic skills he was able to make superb sketches of the objects and from these built wooden replicas which helped him convince others of their dates. Many of his drawings included animals and humans showing, with the help of ropes and pulleys, how our medieval forbearers erected the wooden buildings. In his spare time and possibly for relaxation he painted - these being mainly of trees. However he did not forget his silversmith skills, making objects, drawing them and writing about them and he was also a very good potter.

He liked to smoke a pipe and it no doubt helped him concentrate on his work, he was also interested in poetry and would often quote lines of poetry in discussions. Classical music, reading and watching Shakespeare's plays were also high on his agenda.

Before Cecil appeared on the scene there had been a reluctance to attribute timber buildings that lacked any historical data to a time before the 15th or 16th centuries. So he fought a long lone campaign against those who automatically dated ancient timber buildings to the 15th century, proving on many occasions that various buildings were much older than first thought. His approach was to study the carpenters of the past, their methods, especially joints used, their use of sharp edged tools and established and used a strict datable sequence.

A.C. Edwards an Essex historian and academic became aware of Cecil's work and realised that Cecil needed to write about his work. Edwards took it upon himself to inspire Cecil to write and publish his new ideas which reached Germany, Scandinavia and the U.S.A. and it was not long before he gained world-wide recognition and in fact became a bit of a celebrity. It further resulted in television appearances, notably, 'In search of the Master Carpenters' with Rene Cutforth and the B.B.C. 'Chronicle' series.

Most of his early research was carried out in Essex and an early success was to convince historians that the two barns at Cressing, near Witham were at least two centuries older – dating from the 12th and 13th centuries. This initially raised a storm of controversy, being fuelled by the Times and Daily Telegraph until carbon dating confirmed his view. Professors Horn and Berger said 'Hewett has put ball-bearings under everything'. Following his death a seat was erected at the Cressing barn site and dedicated to him.

A further success was to change the historical understanding of the famous, beautifully carved Paycocke's House at Coggeshall, which had taken its name from John Paycocke, a 16th century wool merchant. It was believed the house was built around 1500, Cecil proved that the house was at least half a dozen buildings fused into one, with some of them dating from the 14th century.

Being a Laindon boy he took great interest in St Nicholas Church and in his book 'Church Carpentry' a study based on Essex examples published in 1974 he dates the roof above the chancel to the early 16th century. Describing it as an important roof, in so far as it affects the evolutionary sequence: Framed in seven cants, with arch-braced collars, side purlins and a collar purlin, a fine example enriched with Tudor-rose relief's as well as with tracery, crenulations and on its wall plates, the 'Honeysuckle' cresting.

He also described the belfry at Laindon as 'another highly complex structure, comprising two timber towers; one of which rises within the other and supports only the bells, while the outer one carries both turret and spire. There is one of the five transverse frames, the central one visible in the North-South section, which seems to echo the 'flowing' style of tracery, while the four posts carrying the bell-frames are combined by straining-beams into 'A' frames.'

There are in excess of 100 timber belfries in Essex depending on how they were defined and categorised. The bell-towers are very much in a minority. Belfries and Bell-towers in particular are some of the most impressive timber structures left to us by the Middle Ages, feats of engineering comparable to the great barns. They had attracted very little attention from antiquaries, architectural historians or archaeologists but Cecil was to go a long way to correct this oversight.

In December 1976 the Hampshire County Council asked him along with a number of other experts: Martin Biddle, director of Winchester research unit, A.C. Barefoot, American scientist and representatives from the Courtauld Institute of Art, Harwell Radio-Carbon Measurement Laboratory and the department of Early Woodwork at the Victoria and Albert Museum to have a look at 'King Arthur's round table'. The table that weighs a ton had hung for centuries on the gable wall of Henry III's Great Hall at Winchester. It was the refurbishment of the Hall that gave Martin Biddle the opportunity to gather the group together to study the table.

Cecil was the first amongst these experts to express the view that the 18ft diameter table was probably made for King Edward 111 early in the 14th Century. He also believed that the paintings of King Arthur and his knights on its surface were probably commissioned by Henry VIII in the 16th Century. To convince the sceptics he built a replica in his garden which he later displayed on television. From this he was able to date the various carpentry techniques. He believed the carpenter was a man who knew about wheels because the table's entire structure was based on the principle of the wheel, with 12 radial arms of wood in its framework, like spokes.

Later X-rays and other age-testing devices were to prove him right and they settled on a date of 1330. Martin Biddle was later to publish a book on the evidence proving the above.

We must be careful not to confuse this table with the Time Team archaeological programme in 2006 which investigated the round table building at Windsor Castle which appears to have been built only a decade later. In these early years of the 14th Century, Round Table Tournaments were held and it seems the building of 200 feet in diameter was built for this purpose. It would appear that it was never finished and fell into disuse within 20 years.

There is no doubt that he loved making his own models, for example he made at least eight harpsichords although he could not play but his wife could.

He made scale models of the buildings destroyed by the great Fire of London 1666. He also confirmed that the long bow that the English dominated the French with during the 100 years' war was made of laburnum and not yew which was used later when there became a shortage of laburnum in this country.

It was in 1980 that Cecil published one of his major works, English Historic Carpentry but it was shortly after this he suffered a severe stroke, which left him unable to communicate but it did not affect his memory. Against all the odds he gradually regained all his faculties; he had always believed that one should work like a 'tightly stretched string' in order to extract the most from one's mind. It might well have been this attitude that brought on his stroke and his final illness. The stroke forced him to retire, although he did make an effort to return to work. Retirement gave him the opportunity to publish yet another book 'English Cathedral and Monastic Carpentry' (1985).

Marjorie (Pat) had a flair for writing poems and has had several published. One of her favourites that has not been published is entitled:

Pictures on the Wall.
27 pictures on the wall many of trees but that's not all.
A few portraits hang on the wall and houses and barns, but that's not all.
A hand-made piece of lace is enclosed in one frame
And one picture is signed by a very famous name,
But experts confirm that this is not true,
Constable did not paint it but they don't know who!
Last but not least hanging on the, The Olde Chantry House,
Established nearly 500 years ago, in the year 1510,
It stands in Billericay High Street, one will never know until when!

24 of the pictures are Cecil's paintings.

Richard acquired his father's carpentry skills and Cecil Junior his drawing skills. Cecil junior travels around South Essex villages and towns sketching and drawing their buildings, 'Ye Olde Chantry House' in Billericay is one of his favourites, I wonder why?

In April of the year just before he died Cecil was awarded an Honorary Doctorate of Technology from the Anglia Polytechnic University. **His work was his hobby.**

Marion Wilberforce..........................Flying Ace

The British Air Transport Auxiliary (ATA) was formed in September 1939. The idea was for pilots, who for various reasons, such as being too old or unfit for RAF service but who were still more than capable to pilot light aircraft. They transported mail, dispatches, medical supplies and later, flying training aircraft fighters, bombers and flying boats from factories to front line squadrons. This enabled the release of desperately needed fully trained pilots for combat duties.

Figure 20 Marion Wilberforce

They were given the nickname 'Ancient and Tattered Airmen'.

What has this to do with Marion Wilberforce? Well! Marion became one of the first of eight women to form the Women's section of the ATA in December 1939. At the time she was living with her husband Robert at their farm, 'Nevendon Manor'.

Marion was born at Boyndlie House, Fraserburgh, Aberdeenshire on 23 July 1902 to John Charles Mathias Ogilvie-Forbes the ninth Laird of Boyndlie and his second wife Anne Marguerite Prendergast.

Marion was educated at home by a succession of French governesses and was obviously fluent in French. By the time she was fourteen she was helping out on the estate by collecting rents from the tenants. At sixteen she was sent off to the Convent of Jesus and Mary at Stony Stratford, Buckinghamshire and then in 1922 she went to Somerville College, Oxford, obtaining a diploma in agriculture in 1925, graduating the following year. While at Oxford she also took a keen interest in sport: she was accomplished in Ju-Jitsu and was a member of the University French Club and Mountaineering Club.

Marion married Robert William Francis Wilberforce who had befriended her brother David at Ampleforth College, Oxford. Robert however was not sure whether he wanted to follow a life as a priest or matrimony so to test his strength he spent six months as a monk at Ampleforth Abbey before deciding against it and at the gate waiting for him was Marion. In the meantime while she was waiting she joined a Field Sports magazine, in addition to travelling widely. In 1931 she visited Quebec, arriving back on 22 July 1932 on the "Duchess of York" just before they married on 3 September 1932. Following the marriage they acquired the Essex farm 'Nevendon Manor' where she kept chickens, bred pigs and cattle. The piglets she named after her brothers, with the runt of the litter being given the name of her youngest brother Malcolm.

Having no children of her own and with her interest and experience in farming she found herself becoming involved in the work of Fairbridge Farm Schools. These were schools set up first in Australia then in Canada by Kingsley Fairbridge and his wife Ruby. It was a charitable organisation set up to help settle orphan children into the agricultural way of life and before she was married she travelled widely, inspecting these farm schools in Australia and Canada. She was for many years Chair of the Child Care Committee and often had children from the school stay with her at Nevendon Manor.

Marion took up flying in 1930, encouraged by her two aviator brothers. She learned to fly at Stag Lane Aerodrome, Edgware where she gained her pilot's licence. Quite an achievement as many women at that time did not even drive motor cars.

She purchased her first aircraft, a de-Havilland Cirrus Moth after investing successfully on the stock exchange. This aircraft she later replaced with a Hornet Moth. She had them registered as farm implements for tax purposes, she used them to transport livestock around. She would take a trip to Europe to visit friends for lunch and bring back chickens or the odd calf placed in bags behind her seat.

Those days instrumentation in aircraft was minimal and navigation was carried out visually. If she got lost she would land and ask the way or read the local signposts. By the time civilian flying ceased in 1939 she had accrued 900 flying hours. So there is no question that by the time war broke out she was a very experienced pilot.

It was because of her piloting experience that she was invited to go to Whitchurch on 16 December for a flight test and was chosen to become one of Pauline Gower's first eight women to join the ATA. She reported for duty at Hatfield No 5 Ferry Pool.

Pauline Gower had been a 'joy ride' pilot during the 1930s and with her partner had started one of the earliest all-women commercial flight businesses.

As war approached and with 2,000 flying hours and 33,000 passengers under her belt she looked for an opportunity to contribute to the war effort.

Even though women had tackled male tasks exceptionally well during the Great War, it was still a male dominated world so it took a lot of persuading but eventually she was granted permission in November 1940 to start up a women's section. Their salary was 20% lower than their male equivalent!

They initially flew light training planes, such as Gipsy and Tiger Moths, from the de Havilland factory at Hatfield to training bases in Northern England and Scotland. However with the loss of Pilots in the Battle of Britain, by the end of 1941 Marion and the others were flying Spitfires, Hurricanes and twin-engine types. She was initially First Deputy but then took over command of No.5 Ferry Pool and in early 1943 she was transferred to No.12 ferry pool, Cosford and took command of the second all-women pool, becoming one of only two women pool commanders in the whole of the ATA. In 1944 she became one of only eleven women allowed to fly four-engine Lancaster and Stirling bombers. Though she would seem quite formidable at first, she was affectionately remembered as being kind and motherly to the younger girls of the ATA Ferry pool.

Figure 21 Spitfire. Ken Porter's collection

The first spitfire she flew was donated by the citizens of Grimsby and was named Grimsby 11.

By June 1940 there were twelve women pilots, which rose to more than 160 by the war's end. One of them was the famous trail blazing Amy Johnson who was killed in January 1941. They became known as the "ATA-girls". At the end of the war Marion had flown over 2400 hours and 100 different aircraft.

She returned to her Essex farm and immersed herself into country life and peacetime flying. Characteristically she declined the offer of an MBE and like many others rarely spoke about her wartime exploits.

While Marion was flying around the skies in her Spitfires her husband Robert served in 134th Field Regiment RA (TA). In his business life he was a solicitor and a partner in Travers, Smith, Braithwaite & Co a corporate law firm. He was also a descendent of William Wilberforce (1759-1833) a leading light in the abolition of slavery.

Marion was described as a 'quintessential "Attagirl" - resourceful, daring and skilled, with more than a touch of eccentricity in her makeup'. So it is not surprising that in peacetime she was best known in aviation as someone who did what she was not supposed to do. Such as skirting the ground at two hundred feet to avoid radar, when flying a route she should not have been on, or disrupting a NATO exercise. She also had little faith in doctors and would obtain her medicines from a vet, claiming her horse was sick.

So there is no doubt that Marion was a very energetic person, full of life and loved adventure. Soon after moving to Nevendon Manor she began hunting and on her return from the war she served on the Essex Union Hunt committee from 1962 to 1982, becoming the only woman master of foxhounds in the Hunt's 236 year history. She was known as a fearless and tough rider. In her seventies she fell into a ditch breaking her collar bone, she re-mounted and completed the hunt before taking herself to hospital. She only stopped hunting in her early eighties after taking another fall and breaking more bones.

In 1947 she became a co-owner of a Hornet Moth G-ADKM with her brother Neil and though the skies became more regulated, Marion continued to fly out of a field at Nevendon Manor, round the British Isles visiting friends in the same happy-go-lucky way of pre-war days. Her post war log book records her slipping in and out of European Countries to have lunch with friends in Luxembourg or listen to music at the Vienna Staatsoper. She took particular pleasure in taking her sister-in-law to Paris to pick up Molyneux culture. On one occasion in May 1949 she set off to visit her brother Neil who was then an air attaché in Moscow. She travelled via Amsterdam, Copenhagen and Stockholm, arriving in Helsinki two days later on the 7th May. To her annoyance she had to leave the aircraft there and go by other means to Moscow. She acquired another Hornet Moth G-AEZG in 1964 and continued her adventures flying until the age of eighty and would have probably continued but for the fact she became disenchanted by all the rules and regulations imposed on the private pilot.

The following is an extract from internet web site 'wordpress':-

'When I was learning to fly at Ipswich Airport in the early 1980s, I can remember an elderly lady flying into the field in an immaculate vintage de Haviland Hornet Moth. She used to come for checks on her flying skills, and also to practice aerobatics in a Cessna 150 Aerobat.

The instructor who flew with her, said she had been a ferry pilot during World War 11 and was one of the best pilots he'd ever sat with.

Searching through the Air Transport Auxiliary, I found this page, which talks about the first eight women pilots of the organisation. This is one of the eight Marion Wilberforce. Marion Wilberforce was an experienced pilot in the 1930s, flying her own Gypsy Moth.

In the ATA she rose to become Deputy Commander of the No. 5 Ferry Pool at Hatfield and later became Commander of the No. 2 Ferry Pool at Cosford. She served the full 5 years until the ATA was disbanded. After the war she purchased a Hornet Moth and continued flying until she was 80. She died at age 93, in July 1996.

I'm absolutely sure, that the pilot was Marion Wilberforce and she was doing aerobatics at an age of almost 80!

Her husband Robert died in December 1984 so she returned to her family home at Boyndlie to live with her brother Malcolm. Though the house was in a state of decay, gardens overgrown and the family chapel derelict they lived happily amongst the decay.

As one would expect she became impatient with physical frailties and refused to wear a hearing aid. She spent her last few months in Stratford Park Nursing Home, Stroud, where she died on the 17 December 1995 at the age of 93. Though she was cremated at Stroud, her ashes were interred at Markington Roman Catholic Church, Harrogate, Yorkshire, near the Wilberforce home.

It is no surprise that Marion took up flying - she really did not have much choice. Her younger brother Neil born 12 December 1900 was commissioned as a Pilot Officer on 1 November 1922 being promoted to Flying Officer on 1 May 1923. He had a long and distinguished career with the Royal Air Force, was awarded the O.B.E. and at his own request retired retaining the rank of Air Vice Marshal on 5 July 1952.

Running a home, a farm, flying, hunting and charity work (Fairbridge Farm Schools) - **What a lady and a Basildon one at that!**

Nevendon Manor is a 16th Century, Grade 11 listed building and was previously known as Broomfords Manor, dating back to at least the early 15th Century. There are the remains of a moat.

Markington Hall – North Yorkshire The family home of the Wilberforce family since 1731. The current Grade 11* listed building was built in approximately 1410 with two wings added in 17th and 18th centuries. A previous hall on the site was built between 1285 and 1309.

Boyndlie House – North Aberdeenshire The family estate of the Ogilvie-Forbes family. The house was built in 1814 and Grade listed C(s).

Figure 22 Nevendon Manor - 2015

Keith Chapman ....'Can he fix it'

Keith was born in Basildon in 1958, initially living in the Kingswood area. The family moved to Plumberow, Lee Chapel North in 1964 and he went to Markhams Chase (now Janet Duke Junior School) School. Martin Fry, organist at St Nicholas Church, Laindon was in the same class as Keith and remembers him as a very bright boy who drew exceptionally well. From there he went to Nicholas Comprehensive (now James Hornsby High School) School.

To earn a few pennies he did an Evening Echo paper round and on Saturdays worked in a Newsagent shop in Laindon Shopping Centre.

He left Basildon when he was 16 as his parents moved to Norfolk to open a pub. He and his brother initially did not want to go but now was glad he did, it really was living the country life and he did summer jobs such as working on the back of a tractor picking potatoes. This was a life that had disappeared from the Basildon area a generation before.

He spent 3 years at Yarmouth College of Art and Design, went back in 2009 to Norwich University College of Arts (NUCA) and accepted an Honorary Degree.

He married his wife Kirsty in May 1984 and Keith made the first sketches of Bob the Builder, with his yellow hard hat and matching digger, before the births of their three boys.

He then spent a few years working with Muppet creator Jim Henson and in 1999 he launched Bob the Builder which is now broadcast to over 240 territories in 45 languages. In Germany he is known as *"Bob der Baumeister"*, Poland as *"Bob Budowniczy"*, in France as *"Bob le Bricoleur"* and in Spain as *"Bob y sus amigos"*.His main characters with Bob are: Wendy, Farmer Pickles, Scoop the Digger, Lofty the Crane, Muck the Digger Dumper, Roly the Roller, Travis the Tractor and Benny the Robo Digger. And the famous catchphrase "Can we fix it" came into being.

Figure 23 Keith Chapman

In the 2008 electoral campaign the future United States President, Barrack Obama adopted the popular slogan "Yes We Can". The question arose did his inspiration come from Bob's catchphrase "Can we fix it...Yes we Can".

When question by a reporter from the Guardian whether he Keith had considered legal action, he jokingly replied *"I don't think so, He's got his finger on the nuclear button and the whole of the US army under his command. I don't want Delta Force coming over my garden wall. He's free to use it as much as he likes."*

In 2000 Bob had a number one hit in the UK singles chart with 'can you fix it' and a year later Bob's adaption of Lou Bega's 'Mambo No 5' also reached number one. There is also a Bob the Builder magazine which is produced fortnightly.

He set up his own business, Chapman Entertainment in 2002 and what followed was: Fifi and the Flowertots and Rory the Racing Car. Fifi is now selling in 160 territories worldwide. Bob is voiced by Neil Morrissey and Roary the Racing Car by Stirling Moss, Murray Walker and Peter Kay. Other creation Raa Raa the Noisey lion, is voiced by Lorraine Kelly.

Bob in its first ten years generated worldwide income of $5bn. Keith, though no longer holds the rights but does pick up handsome royalties and is a Multi-Millionaire in his own right. Not bad for a lad who went to James Hornsby High School, Laindon.

Unfortunately in 2012 Chapman Entertainment went into administration and was sold to Hit Entertainment (Henson International Television) who are one of the world's leading pre-school entertainment companies. Subsequently Keith has set himself up as Keith Chapman Production and has continued to be heavily involved in pre-school animation.

Chapter 3 - Entertainment

Joan Marion Sims..............................Actress

Whenever you talk to people in Laindon about famous people the first person that comes to mind is Joan Sims, our Joan as I have heard said many times.

Joan died on the 28th June 2001 at the age of 71. She had been admitted into Chelsea Hospital where she died holding the hand of her lifelong friend Norah Holland another Carry on Star.

Her funeral was held at Putney Vale Crematorium on 5 July 2001. A Memorial service was held at St. Paul, Covent Garden (commonly known as the Actors' Church) on 22 October 2001. Her ashes were scattered at Putney Vale Cemetery, London.

A plaque dedicated to her memory was unveiled where she lived at Thackeray Street, Kensington, London in September 2002 by Barbara Windsor. She was joined by other

Figure 24 Joan Sims - Photograph by Derick Pope

stars of the classic Carry On film series including Liz Fraser. A celebratory lunch followed the unveiling which included many other old friends, including John Inman.

Peter Rogers, producer-director of the 'Carry on Series of Films' said from his office at Pinewood studios that: 'She was a lovely, lovely lady and a wonderful actress. How many laughs we had together. She will be sadly missed by very many people'.

Following her death, surviving Carry On stars celebrated her achievement in the Carry On films. Barbara Windsor had this to say: "To me she was the last of the great Carry On's, she was there at the beginning. Her talent was wonderful, she could do any accent, dialect, she could dance, sing, play dowdy and glam. We laughed all the time and giggled a lot. I will sorely miss her."

It is no doubt that she was a very versatile actress and could play many parts, she was never typecast like so many other actors and actresses.

On the 9th May 2005 on what would have been her 75th birthday a memorial plaque was unveiled at Laindon railway station. Joan was born in the station house. Her father John Henry Sims was the station master, he had joined the LMS (London, Midland and Scottish Railways) as a booking clerk, after leaving the army at the end of the First World War. He had served in Malta and

Figure 25 Plaque on Laindon Station Wall. Ken Porter's photograph.

seen action in the trenches with the City of London Regiment.

Laindon at this time was a little community on its own, being just one of the stops on the Fenchurch Street to Shoeburyness line. Today it has more or less been swallowed up by Basildon.

Joan was born, Irene Joan Marion Sims, in the station house, Laindon and she was one hundred percent 'Essex Girl', both her parents were Essex born and bred. Laindon Station was to become her playground. From a very early age she had a passion for performing. If she was not play acting in the station house, she could be found in the ladies waiting room or loading bays in the goods yard where she would dress up and perform for the many travellers. Her father was not very amused by her antics; it was still a time when children and little girls in particular should be seen and not heard. So her father was even less pleased when she played a wind-up-gramophone given to her by an old lady to enhance her performances. Many occasions came the cry 'Joan-indoors'.

Although Laindon station was quite a family affair, her Aunt Edith served in the sweet and tobacco kiosk, life there for young Joan was rather lonely and as she went to St John's a private school in Billericay and later to Brentwood High School for Girls it meant she had very few close friends.

It's hard to believe but Joan was basically a shy person so it appears rather strange that she was so willing to dress up and perform. Was it a make believe life she was creating for herself to make up for the loneliness and lack of friends. Well she had a captive audience in the passengers and therefore many characters she could mimic. Mimicking was to become one of her specialities in her professional life.

Joan went on Sundays to the local Methodist Sunday School in Langdon Hills. It was not to her liking so she would occasionally dodge going and disappear to the local recreation ground with a few other like-minded girls.

The Radion cinema however was one of her favourite haunts on a Saturday morning where her dreams of becoming an actress were hatched. She particularly loved the musicals.

Figure 26 Laindon and District Operatic Society. Ken Porter's collection

The cinema frequently held talent shows and at one of the shows Joan sang 'Oh what a Beautiful Morning' from Oklahoma. Joan's first official acting role possibly came in her early teens when she volunteered to act as a wounded casualty for the 'Glee Club' (St John's Ambulance brigade). Like many girls of her age she joined the local Girl Guides pack and was thrilled when she was of the Blue Tit Patrol....to which in later life amongst the Carry On Crew she would have the mickey taken out of her. It was around this time that she also started to get serious in drama and joined the Langdon Players, the Laindon Amateur Operatic Society and the Youth Centre Drama group. (Laindon High Road School).

The Youth Centre Drama group in 1946 entered the South East Essex Drama Festival at Walthamstow with a short play 'Lonesome Like'. Joan played a mill hand and was awarded the best Individual Performance of the Festival. This helped her to make up her mind that it was a stage career she would like.

It took her four attempts to get into RADA (Royal Academy of Dramatic Art in Bloomsbury). In the end it was a letter from her father enclosing cuttings of reviews from the local paper and a third term at PARADA (RADA preliminary academy) that saw her being admitted to RADA. It was the Essex Education Committee that had supported Joan in the way of a grant but she also supplemented her income by working in the C & A department store in Oxford Street. She won the £10 Mabel Temperley prize for grace and charm of movement while at RADA.

In 1940 Doris Tranter opened a hairdressing business in Laindon High Road and it was here that Joan while at RADA would attended to have her hair styled.

It was the living in and around Laindon Station, the school mistress in Brentwood and customers she came across while working at C & A that provided her with endless material for future acting roles. Joan was 22 when she finally left Laindon to make her mark in the entertainment world. She did return in the early 1970s to open a fete but never returned after that.

The Wickford Times on 26 October 1951 reported that her versatile voice was chosen to speak lines of several characters in one of the latest series of children's programmes, "Vegetable Village". A previous article in the Wickford Times reports one of her first parts in a children's program on the television where she plays a maid in the play 'John of the Fair'. The report goes on the say 'Miss Sims, a "born" comedienne, has a natural gift for humorous characters.' There is a photograph in the paper showing her on a bicycle with a caption stating 'She is very much a home girl and she always cycles for her mother's shopping.'

She went on to appear in 100 motion pictures and television productions:
- Love among the Ruins, starring Laurence Olivier and Kathrine Hepburn.
- Doctor at Sea, starring Dirk Bogarde and Brigitte Bardot
- As time goes by, with Judy Dench
- On the up, with Dennis Waterman
- Till death do us Part.
- Only Fools and Horses.

and of course twenty four Carry On Films where she played alongside of Sidney James; Kenneth Williams; Kenneth Connor; Hattie Jacques; Charles Hawtrey; Jim Dale; Terry Scott; Bernard Bresslaw; Peter Butterworth, Frankie Howard and of course Barbara Windsor.

She had a number of relationships, Tyrone Power and Sid James to name but two but she never married and drunk too much at times especially after the death of her friend Hattie Jacques. Though she did receive a proposal from Kenneth Williams, he said 'we will be the talk of the town.'

As stated Joan was a very private person, very rarely gave interviews and kept away from the press but on occasions they did get the odd comment:
- *'I was always being ticked off for making the class laugh, usually by mimicking the teacher'*.
- *'I don't think I've ever had anybody say the words, 'Will you marry me?' not even someone tight as a tick at a party'*.
- *'To be a comic women, you have to put up with a bit of banter, but I didn't mind. I've got a dirty sense of humour and I never found those things offensive'*.
- *'I was once mistaken for Shirley MacLaine in a fish and chip shop off the Edgware Road*
- *'I had not expected to end up on my own in a small flat'* (the most she ever received for a carry on film was £3000).

She said her motivation for acting was a child's desire to please, she certainly did that and the people of Laindon will never forget her.

If you want to read more about Joan Sims, she published her own biography 'High Spirits' in 2000.

Joe Goodman........Comedian-King of the one liners

Figure 27 Joe Goodman - By kind permission of Jo Goodman

Joan was loved so was our Joe.

Eve to Adam: "Do you love me?"
Adam: "I haven't much of a choice, have I."

Husband, just home from work, says to his wife
"There is a black cat in the Kitchen. That's lucky isn't it?"
Wife: "That one is it's just eaten your dinner."

Just a couple of one liner's from the undisputed "King of the one-liners" and yes he is one of ours, a thoroughbred, Dunton and Laindonite, 'Joe Goodman'.

Again many of you might say who? But those of you who watched 'The

Comedians, Granada Television' during the 1980's (second series) or who have been active in the sporting world, might well have come across him and I am sure you would agree he is the King of the one Liners.

"I asked my bank manager to check my balance. He pushed me over!"

Those of you who lived in the Dunton Plotland area during the 1940/50's would have known him as Joey Cotterill. Joe was born at Rochford Hospital in February 1939 and abandoned six weeks later in a wet pram in a shop doorway in Laindon High Road. (Possibly Churchill Johnson's) As his mother Annie walked away distressed, a lady nearby, by the name of Ethel Thomas asked what the matter was and agreed to look after him for a few weeks until Annie sorted herself out.

Ethel lived with her husband Henry and their three teenagers, in a small plotland bungalow called 'Clearview' with a bell tent and an outside toilet. The bungalow was in Stacey Drive, part of the area we now know as Dunton Plotlands.

Ethel immediately got in touch with the Essex Child Welfare, who gave her ten shillings a week for Joe's upkeep. By the time Joe's mother got back in touch several months later, there were another six fostered children in tow. As Joe said *"You don't see storks like that these days"*.

Joe was to stay with Ethel, who became his foster mum and for the next sixteen years he lived in the plotland area moving from one wooden bungalow to another with foster children coming and going. When it was time for bed he never knew whether he was going to sleep in the bell tent, attic, or Anderson air raid shelter Ethel had bunkered out. Most of the bungalows had outside 'Bucket and Chuck it' toilet arrangements; water was either rain water, water from wells or stand pipes. Calor gas lighting, heating normally by coal fires or paraffin stoves. Cooking was done on a coal or wood burning Belling oven. Ethel was a very good cook but Joey always sat either on his own or with other fostered children in the scullery eating their meals, never with the family.

Ethel was a very strict but hard working woman; however like everybody else living in the area the whole family had to join in with the chores of the day. So every day you would see locals going about their business looking after the gardens, collecting water or carrying their shopping from Laindon across the fields and unmade roads.

Joe vividly remembered he would have to go and collect water from a nearby stand pipe and when he became big and strong enough, a 'yoke' was placed on his shoulders for him to be able to carry two pails of water. A key was needed to unlock the door of a concrete box to get at the stand pipe. While waiting for the slow running water to fill the buckets he would stand on the box and sing *"Rag time cowboy Joe"* or *"I'm going to buy myself a paper doll"*

Although life was hard it was also fun with plenty to do in the country, the experience is possibly the reason why Joe had such a sense of humour and was able to use it to entertain people.

He was not to see his mother again until 1947 when he went to see a Mrs Cotterill and her children David, John, Ann and Milly. He did not meet his family again until 2003, when David informed him that his mother had died in 1964.

Joe initially went to Dunton Junior School, and then transferred to Langdon Hills Junior School before moving on to the Laindon High Road Secondary School. It was not long before the school children nicknamed him 'Cotton reel'. A little upsetting at first but he looked back on it with some affection.

It was while at Laindon High Road in 1954 at the age of 15 when he had his first stage experience. Two amateur play writers by the names of Bill Slade and Harold Greaves had bought a bungalow nearby called 'Landview' and they asked Joe if he would like to play the part of the cat in 'Dick Whittington' for the St John Glee Party.

There were many drama and variety clubs in Laindon in the days before the New Town of Basildon and the St John Glee Club was one of them; they were part of Laindon's St John's Ambulance Brigade. Joe got a standing ovation for his part and this is what the local paper had to say: "Dick Whittingham was played by Jean Scott, but Joey Cotterill made such an appealing white-faced cat it would be a crime to relegate him (or is it her?) to the bottom of the cast list" – He was on his way!

He was a prefect at Laindon High Road School and also joined the St Nicholas Church choir. There is, however, no doubt that he was a bit of a lad but if anything was wanted it was Joey they sent for. The School on one occasion wanted a horse for a pageant, so off he went and spoke to a local farmer Jack Buckenham and asked if he could borrow old Henry, Jack obliged and Joe played King John riding old Henry.

I said to my wife "let me bet on one more horse and it will be the last" **IT WAS.**

By now Joe was singing and performing in the many talent shows that went on in Laindon and on one occasion won 7 shillings and six pence at St Mary's Church Hall, Langdon Hills.

He left School in 1955 and started work as a shipping clerk in the city, soon afterwards he moved into lodgings in Thundersley. However entertaining was obviously in his blood so he continued performing at talent shows and was acting as M.C. at Social Clubs, singing and dancing, earning £5 per night.

His big break came when after winning various heats at the Butlins Holiday Talent shows; he won the final at the New Victoria Theatre, London in 1969. Won Opportunity Knocks, compared by Hughie Green in 1970, Voted Club Entertainer of the year 1972 and Southern Entertainer in the same year.

His lists of credits are now endless; performing in four Royal shows at the Palladium and Theatre Royal, Windsor. Performing for Princess Diana, Buckingham Palace garden Parties, The British Music Hall, The Variety Club, Golf, Cricket Boxing evenings, conferences and exhibitions. He was a proud

Figure 28 Joe meeting Prince Charles. By kind permission of Joe Goodman

member of the Grand Order of Water Rats.

A boxer was getting such a good hiding both eyes were cut and swollen, blood was dripping from his mouth and his nose was broken. At the end of the first round, his manager consoled him as he applied the necessary medication and said "Don't worry you're going great on radio, the commentator's a friend of mine!"

One of his most memorable performances was during the Kosovo conflict when he performed on five ships in two days, going by helicopter from one ship to another, Ark Royal being one of the ships.

In 2003 he decided to look his real family up, he found David living in Basildon, needless to say it was an emotional reunion. David informed him that John was living in Ramsgate, Kent. John it turns out was in the same business as Joe and worked as a Redcoat at Butlins during the 1960's and 70's, no doubt their paths had met without realising it. Joe went on to meet Ann, Millie had passed away and a further sister he did not know he had, Gwen who informed him that she and her daughter had been trying to trace him on the internet. As Joe pointed out the reason they could not find him was possibly because in 1957 he changed his name by deed Poll, thinking that 'Goodman' would be a more suitable name for an entertainer.

I first met Joe at Three Rivers Golf Club, Cold Norton many years ago, he was there as guest of honour at either a Golf or Cricket function and being a cricket fanatic the joke he told the guests has always stayed with me:

'The unfortunate cricketer had been given out LBW by the umpire, he threw his bat down, ran across the pitch and confronted the gentleman wearing the white coat, declaring that it wasn't LBW and you should get yourself a pair of glasses. Who then replied...I should get a pair of glasses! I'm selling ice cream!!

Joe passed away on the 28th April 2014, he had been suffering with Leukaemia for some time but only a month or so before he was performing at the Cliffs Pavilion, Westcliff-on-Sea. His funeral was held on the 23rd May at Southend-on-Sea Crematorium. The place was packed out, standing room only. His service sheet said 'A Celebration of the Life of Joe Goodman' and what a celebration it was. The service was conducted by Canon Roger Royle who used to present Songs of praise for BBC One and other television and radio productions. Roger de Courcy, Russ Conrad plus many other fellow comedians and members of the Water Rats were there.

The Entrance music was 'Thank you for the years – by Shirley Bassey' Hymns that followed were 'All things bright and beautiful' and 'Jerusalem' with the final music being' I'll be seeing you by Rod Stewart'

It was a comedy show in itself but as his wife Maureen said that is the way he would have wanted it.

There is no doubt that Joe was one of this country's best comedians and was very much in a league of his own. He had the ability to improvise at venues both large and small. He often invited the audience to give him any subject and he will fire back a joke about it. He was at ease with all types of audiences, Male, Female or mixed not a problem to our Laindon Joe.*'Grandson says to his grandmother while being driven to school, nanny where's all the gits, prats and dickheads gone? Oh, they only come out when your granddad drives'.*

He was a happy family man who surprisingly found time to pursue his hobbies of Golf, painting and inventions. He designed his own props and he still found time each year to go back to his roots. On Boxing Day 2013 following the publication of his autobiography 'Is anybody out there' he was interviewed live by BBC Essex and took the young interviewer back to his plotland home of Dunton.

Figure 29 Joe at launch of the Laindon & District Community Archive at Laindon Library. Ken Porter's Photograph

He used to turn up every year at the Dunton reunion and keep everybody in stitches with his new jokes or stories of life amongst the Plotland pioneers, sending everybody away on a high. If not busy he would also come along and open any local event. He was guest of honour at Laindon Reunion at Laindon High Road School a few years before the school was demolished. In 2008 he opened St Nicholas Church, Laindon's fete entitled 'Laindon has Talent' and in 2010 appeared at Laindon Library to launch the 'Laindon and district Community Archive' web site. No wonder we all loved him.

Plenty more could be said but if you want to know more about his life why not get his book 'Is anybody out there' and true to form all profits from sales are for the Bud Flanagan Leukaemia Fund.

Remember if laughter is the milestone of your journey, then depend on it and you'll never get lost'. That's our King.

Figure 30 By kind permission of Joe Goodman

Joan Dowling ....Laindon's tragic child star

I was aware of Joan but until I read Paul Sticklands piece on the Laindon and District Community Archive web site did not appreciate that she had a connection with Laindon.

Paul has kindly allowed me to reproduce his article with a few additions:

"Laindon had two famous Joan's, who were close contemporaries. Joan Sims of "Carry on" fame, and Joan Dowling child star of "Hue and Cry", the first of the Ealing comedies. She went on to star in numerous plays, pantomimes and about 20 films, before tragedy struck at the age of 26.

Figure 31 Joan Dowling

Joan Dowling was the illegitimate daughter of Vera Martin of Upton Park. When the unmarried Vera became pregnant, she was sent to her maternal grandmother, who had lived in Laindon since the early 1920s. Unfortunately she never knew her father.

Joan was born on the 8th January 1928 at the house called Carlyle, which is one of the turreted bungalows in the High Road North. During this time she had her first taste of "stardom" by winning a talent show at a circus in Laindon. As far as I have been able to ascertain, she lived there until she was 7 or 8, at which time she moved to Uxbridge.

She had a passion for acting and dreamed of becoming an actress but the family were too poor to afford her acting lessons, therefore she was never formally trained but took roles in small plays, pantomimes and other productions whenever she could. At the age of 14, she approached a London acting agency and was given her first 'proper' part in a small production (title unknown). Her major acting debut came when producer Anthony Hawtrey cast her in the role of Norma Bates in the Joan Temple play 'No Room at the Inn' The play's first performance was at the Embassy Theatre in July 1945. Subsequently the play transferred under producer Robert Atkins to the Winter Garden Theatre, Drury Lane. She received rave reviews for her performance, resulting in a talent scout spotting her and offering her a long term movie contract. She also played the same role in the 1948 film version, with the screenplay co-written by the famous Welsh author Dylan Thomas and Ivan Foxwell. She signed her first film contract at the age of 17 for Associated British Pictures.

This link is to a very interesting Pathe' newsreel, made at the start of her career.

http://www.britishpathe.com/video/a-star-in-the-making#

She went on to star in several films, including Train of Events, with Jack Warner and Valerie Hobson and Murder without a Crime, with Dennis Price and Derek Farr.

She was perhaps best known for her role as the tomboy Clarry in the 1947

Ealing Studios production 'Hue and Cry' a story set among the rubble and buildings of post-war London about a group of school children who discover that crooks have been sending coded messages about upcoming jobs to their gang using the pages of a children's comic. It was on the set she met another cast actor Harry Fowler, they fell in love and were married on the 15 September, 1951.

Joan and Harry were the "Posh & Becks" of their era, a glamorous young couple who were seen at all the film premieres and major social events of the early fifties.

She continued to get small roles in films like Landfall and Pool of London, she also worked on radio in-addition to several more plays such as 'Murder without a Crime' 'Robinson Crusoe' and 'A Midsummer Night's Dream' as Puck.

Other credits:

Films: - Bond street (1948), A Man's Affair (1949), for them that Trespass (1949), The magic Box (1951), 24 Hours of a Women's Life (1952), Women of Twilight (1952).

Joan was heartbroken when she discovered her husband was having an affair and on 31 March 1954 the twenty-six year old actress committed suicide. She was found unconscious in the gas filled kitchen in her West London home. Her official cause of death was suicide by asphyxiation. Joan was cremated and buried at Golders Green Crematorium, London, England. Her mother and other relatives believe that her death may have been accidental. They think that she was only attempting suicide to scare her husband. Harry Fowler eventually remarried and passed away in 2012.

At the time she was on Radio in 'Meet the Huggetts' and she was replaced after her death by Vera Day.

A very sad end to a very promising career. Who knows what she might have achieved. As a vivacious actress of the cockney type, it is easy to imagine her in "Carry on" type roles. Perhaps alongside Joan Sims, her Laindon contemporary. I have found no evidence that the two Joan's knew

ACTRESS FOUND DEAD

LAINDON-born Miss Joan Dowling (26), the actress, of Farmer Street, Kensington, died after being found unconscious in a gas-filled room at her home on Wednesday.

Miss Dowling was the daughter of a Laindon builder's labourer.

After three years of small parts she achieved fame almost overnight with a portrayal of the cockney evacuee child in "No Room at the Inn," at the Embassy Theatre, Swiss Cottage.

Then she went into films first in "Hue and Cry," and then a screen version of "No Room at the Inn." Other films she made included "The Magic Box," "24 Hours of a Woman's Life," and "Women of Twilight."

She was the youngest star at the Royal Film Performance in November 1949, attended by the King and Queen.

While making "Hue and Cry," she met actor Harry Fowler, who once sold newspapers in Piccadilly Circus. They were married in 1951.

Police are satisfied there was no foul play.

Figure 32 Basildon Standard April 3rd 1954

each other, but it seems likely that they may have done.

Joan's mother, Vera Martin was my mother's sister and therefore Joan was my first cousin, a fact of which I am very proud."

Genevieve Alison Moyet...........Singer-Songwriter

Genevieve Alison was born in Billericay hospital on the 18th June 1961 to Doris her English mother and Michel her French father. The family were living at the time in Butneys Road in the Ghyllgrove area. She has an older brother Clifford and sister Jeanne.

Figure 33 Alison Moyet

Doris loved the French language and in 1953 answered an advert in a newspaper offering a post as an 'au pair' in Cognac. It was during her year's stay that she met Michel who returned to England with her, where they were married in London in August 1954. They returned to France but after four years they returned to England but it is not surprising that the family spent long summer holidays camping in France and staying with Michel's parents.

The family moved to Little Lullaway, Lee Chapel North where she went to Janet Duke Primary School (previously Markham's Chase). It was at Janet Duke's, like most children that she learned to play the recorder and at the same time she taught herself the flute, piano and even managed to perform one song on the mouth-organ. All three of the children went to the Methodist Church Sunday School in Ballards Walk, Lee Chapel North.

In 1971 the family moved again to Laindon High Road North, where her mother, Doris still lives, her father having died in 2014. Although Doris taught French at Laindon High Road School, Alison actually went to Nicholas Comprehensive School (now James Hornsby High School) in St Nicholas Lane, Laindon, leaving at the age of 16.

At the school she was in the same year as Martin Gore and Andrew Fletcher, future members of Depeche Mode. On leaving school Alison began a music foundation course at Southend College of Technology but quit when she failed the theory. More musical studies followed in London where she also became a proficient piano tuner. She also worked for a time for the cosmetic company Yardley's in Basildon.

Her father's interest was rugby so in her early years she was often seen around the Basildon Rugby Club, however she soon transferred her allegiance and became a lifelong supporter of Southend United Football Club. For many years she could be found in the West Stand at Roots Hall. In fact part of the Video for 'Is this love' was filmed at the ground. Also her song the 'Blue' was used as the theme tune of the British TV series 'Playing the Field', it was her ode to her love of football and of Southend United.

She admits to being part of the Basildon and Canvey punk scene where she performed on the pub rock circuit. One of her first songs she sung was 'That Ol' Devil Called Love' and because of this she became known for the next twenty years as a Jazz singer, although she admits she did not know anything about Jazz. The first group she formed was the Vandals' with school friends Kim Forey, Sue Pager and guitarist Robert Allen and the first time they performed was at The Grand Hotel, Leigh-on-Sea on 14 April 1978 This was followed by many local performances at the Woodlands Youth Centre in Kingswood, Van Gogh's in Paycock Road and at the Bandstand in Gloucester Park, but after a year the group split and Alison replaced Mike Maynard as vocalist for the 'Vicars'.

In the short time she was with them they performed at the Double Six pub in Basildon, Southend College of Technology and the Shrimpers Club. She then formed another rhythm and blues band called 'The Screaming Ab Dab's' but like the rest this was only short lived as she met up with Vince Clarke and they formed the 'Yazoo' in 1981 and their first record 'Only You' went to number two in the charts. Their first album 'Upstairs at Erics' went platinum in 1982.

After two albums and several singles they split and Alison went solo and her first album, entitled 'Alf' a nickname she had received at school was released in November 1984. The album went Quadruple platinum, spending two years in the charts and sold over 1.5 million copies in U.K alone. At some point on leaving home she lived on the Heathleigh estate in Langdon Hills.

In 1985 and again in 1988 she was awarded the Best British Female Solo Artist. In 1985 she appeared on stage twice with Bob Geldof and a range of stars in the Live Aid Concert. This was followed in 1987 with her album 'Rain dancing ' and this was another tremendous success. More followed, with a single from 'Hoodoo', 'It Won't Be Long' received a Grammy nomination for Best Female Rock Performer.

Then in 1994 she released the album 'Essex' and this was going to be her last for eight years. In 2001 she appeared at the London's Adelphi as 'Mama Morton' in the stage show 'Chicago' alongside Denise Van Outen for six months. In 2005 she performed with Dawn French in a stage show 'Smaller' which first did the regional rounds before a stint at the London Lyric.

Alison and Dawn played two sisters whose mother was disabled. While Alison's character was singing in bars on Spain's Costa Del Sol, Dawn's role was that of a school teacher who was also responsible for caring for the sisters' mother. Alison wrote the music for the show, in which she also sang.

Figure 34 Alison Moyet & Vice Clarke

Alison's record contract was with Sony but in 2002 she was released and she signed up with Sanctuary Records, releasing her fifth album 'Hometime' that went Gold, earning her nominations for both Brit Award and the Mercury Prize.

2008 saw her team up again with Vince for a 'Yazoo' Reconnected Tour. This was quickly followed by a solo tour of the U.S and Canada (16 dates) with another ten in the U.K in 2009.

On the 26 September 2014 at the Cliffs Pavilion, Westcliff, Alison received an honorary degree from the University of Essex for her contributions to British Music, she said: "I am exceedingly proud to be awarded this. Southend Technical College provided an education which was available to all.

It gave me the invaluable opportunity to better understand music and explore the arts to meet people who would inform my choices and also gave a platform on which to perform."

She is still touring and in 2014 following an exhausting tour around Britain which included a date at the Cliffs Pavilion in Southend she also gave 25 interviews in 2 weeks.

This was after being housebound for years with agoraphobia, caused she believes by being accidentally rude in person to fellow singer Elvis Costello after one of his shows. She says that it was her husband David Ballard that helped her recovery. It was on the programme Desert Island Discs in May 2014 that she revealed all including smashing all her gold discs and wiping clean her computer. She was obviously giving herself a fresh start and her first album after returning to her music was 'Minutes'.

Other than this confession she has managed to keep her private life fairly private, she has been married twice and has three children Joe, Alex and Caitlin and is currently living in Brighton.

She has now sold over 20 million records and as one reporter said' you can take the Girl out of Essex but you can't take the Essex out of the Girl.' I would like to change Essex to Laindon.

Denise Van Outen...............Actress and Presenter

Denise's own website refers to her as 'The First Lady of Essex' but for me I would like to refer to her as to-days 'First Lady of Basildon'.

Denise Outen was born on 27 May 1974 in Basildon Hospital and it was not long afterwards that the family moved to nearby Stanford-le-Hope. So I am quite happy for Stanford-le-Hope to have a little bit of her but to the rest of us she is a good old Basildon girl.

Similar to our Joan Sims a showbiz career was in her blood because at the tender age of seven she was putting on shows for her neighbours and modelling knitting patterns.

Her parents Ted and Kathleen Outen came from council-house roots, with her mother being a child carer and her father a Tilbury-Docker/security-guard, she was the youngest of three, Brother Terry and Sister Jackie. In Stanford-le-Hope she went to Joseph's Roman Catholic School and had joined the Susan Stephen's Theatre School in Corringham to learn dance, ballet, tap and modern.

At the age of 12 she joined the Sylvia Young Theatre School in Marylebone, London and paid her fees from income earned from modelling and television commercials and by then she had already appeared in the stage production of *Les Miserables* playing the part of Eponine and appearing in *A-*

Midsummer Night's Dream with the Royal Shakespeare Company.

As a teenager she had brief roles in a number of television dramas such as The Bill and by now she had added Van to her name as she thought it sounded more interesting, whether there is any Dutch blood in her is unknown.

Figure 35 Denise Van Outen

While at Sylvia Young's she had to catch the 6am bus from Basildon and to help out financially she took some professional singer roles mainly backing vocals. One such group was with Melanie Blatt with the band Dreadzone, and Sang also with Cathy Warwick in the girl group called *Those 2 Girls,* She was slowly becoming an all-rounder.

Television seemed to like her and at twenty-one came her first big break when she co-presented *The Big Breakfast* with Johnny Vaughan, her role mainly being the attractive and cheeky weather and travel reporter and by the end of the 1990s they had become quite a hit.

She left *Big Breakfast* in late 1998 and there followed a few ups and downs, *Something for the Weekend* on Channel 4 was not too successful. In 1999 in addition to several episodes of *The Bill, Murder in Mind* and other television programmes she was voted Rear of the Year.

Denise kept picking up parts, appearing in the crime comedy film, *Love, Honour and Obey*, romantic comedy *Are you Ready for Love,* then in 2001 she was back in the West End playing Roxie Hart in the hit musical *Chicago* at the Adelphi Theatre which proved a great hit amongst the theatregoers. She then went off to Broadway with the musical before returning to the show in London in April 2002. Guest appearances in the show *The Play What I Wrote* followed in the same year. Denise was now in great demand, she could sing, act and dance. She was back on the West End stage in 2003 with Andrew Lloyd Webber's one-woman show *Tell Me on a Sunday* which he reworked for her, It was a great success. This was soon followed by being one of the lead characters in the ITV sentimental drama *Where the Heart Is*. It ran for two series

Her credits continued:
- 2007 played Maureen in *Rent Remixed*.
- 2008 Denise was reunited with Johnny Vaughan as co-host *of Capital Breakfast* for Capital Radio. Vaughan appeared to be jealous of her and she left the show after six months. He has not spoken to her since.
- 2008, *Who Dares Sings!* As co-presenter
- 2009, played Paulette in West End production of *Legally Blonde*
- July 2009, played Mary in *Hotel Babylon* for BBC
- August 2009, made her Edinburgh Festival Debut *in Blondes*
- 2010, she appeared alongside Neil Morrissey in the film *Run for your Wife*
- 2010, Narrator for *The Only Way is Essex*.
- 2011, starring role in the film *Run for your Wife* with Dame Judi Dench
- 2011, TV judge – *Born to Shine* – to raise money for Save the Children.
- 2013, she turned her hand to writing and co-wrote with Terry Ronald the one women musical play *Some Girl I Used To Know*
- 2013, Denise presented her own Saturday afternoon show on London Magic 105.4

The list of credits is endless and in between she has followed up her success as Roxie in America by being on the panel for the reality show *Any Dream Will Do* following her success on the British version. One of her odd jobs was being a judge for the *Miss World* contest in Poland in 2006. This was followed in 2007 with Denise topping the poll to find the most desired *bikini body* in a poll of readers of Grazia magazine.

In September 2012 she faced one her biggest challenges by appearing in *Strictly Come Dancing*, she was partnered by professional dancer James Jordan. Unfortunately there was some criticism because of her stage and dance experience. She eventually came runner-up with Kimberley Walsh behind the winner gymnast Louis Smith.

We must not forget her singing career whereby she has released a number of singles:
- 1994 *Wanna Make You Go. Uuh* with Those 2 Girls reached No. 74 in the charts
- 1995 *All I Want* with Those 2 Girls...reaching No. 36 in the charts
- 2002 *Can't Take My Eyes Off You* with Andy Williams, reaching No. 23
- etc

Like many female celebrities she has dabbled in the fashion business, designing to date two collections. A maternity range and an autumn, winter collection. This leads us on to her marriage to Lee Mead winner of the British version of *Any Dream Will Do* in the Seychelles in April 2009 and their baby daughter Betsy, born in May 2010. In exchange for donations to The Louis Dundas Centre at Great Ormond Street Hospital they allowed one official photo release to the publications. Unfortunately the couple split in July 2013 but still remain good friends.

Other relationships included dating (1998-2001) and becoming engaged to Jay Kay lead singer of *Jamiroquai*. Following their split he released an album *A Frank Odyssey* which was mostly about their break-up.

While starring in the role Legally Blonde she wrote a book about her experiences of pregnancy called *Bumpalicious*, which was published in March 2011 and has since written another called *Adventures in Parenthood*. In addition to her two books she has written a monthly column for Prima magazine and has written articles for the online parenting magazine *Mumazine* founded by her close friend Sam Mann. You can read her articles at_www.mumazine.com._

Her latest venture will be in BBC one soap 'EastEnders' and the Basildon Echo headlines read when the news broke were: '*Sparks fly in the Square as Denise joins Eastenders*'. Denise said "I'm really excited to be joining EastEnders as I've been a fan of the series for years. This year marks the show's 30th anniversary, so it feels even more special to be part of the celebration."

Executive producer, Dominic Treadwell-Collins added: "it was only a matter of time before Denise Van Outen walked on to Albert Square."

Josh James Dubovie (James) .Laindon Sensation

'OSLO HERE I COME'

'*Singing sensation Josh Dubovie won the hearts of the public on Friday and was picked to represent the UK in the 2010 Eurovision Song Contest.*'

'*Since blowing the judges away with an amazing vocal performance of Jason Donovan's 'Two Many Hearts in the World' live on BBC1, the 19 year-old from Laindon has been thrust into the spotlight and is loving every minute of it.*'
Essex Enquirer, 18 March 2010.

His parents Richard and Kim were naturally very proud of their son and Richard reported to the *Enquirer* '*I was always telling him to get a proper job, but now look at him! He'll be the one that's bringing home the bacon now.*'

The BBC show was 'Your Country Needs You' hosted by Graham

Norton, the amazing thing was that the following day he received a rejection letter from 'Britain's Got Talent' following a previous rejection letter from the 'X Factor'.

Figure 36 Josh James

In an interview with Basildon Echo he said *'I really hope I can do Laindon, Basildon, Essex and the UK proud in the Eurovision Song Contest.'* The song he sung was "That Sounds Good to Me" written by writers and producers Mike Stock and Pete Waterman. Well he did us proud but unfortunately he came last but as we know it is now a strange contest. Josh was born on the 27 November 1990 in the Southend area but the family moved to Worthing Road when he was only a few months old. He went to Merrylands Junior School, Laindon before moving onto Billericay Senior School where he completed his A-levels in Music Technology, Drama and English Literature. Naomi Phillips, Josh's former drama teacher, said: "I am not surprised at Josh's success. He was always such an amazing performer, but he's also a lovely down to earth person. He discovered he could sing at about 14 and he hasn't looked back since."

Before he discovered he could sing he joined at the age of nine Stage Ability, an after school stage club resulting in him appearing in a number of episodes of 'Hollyoaks'. Drama was obviously in his blood from an early age and at 15 he played Enjoras in a school production of *Les Miserable*.

2008 was a busy year for Josh, he won the Blues Idol competition, Billericay's Got Talent and the Voice of St Lukes Hospice, Basildon contest. He is the first Celebrity Patron of St Lukes and has promised to participate in their events for the foreseeable future.

Since returning from Norway he has been kept extremely busy, in January 2011 he appeared at the Civic Hall, Grays in the pantomime 'Aladdin'. 'Sleeping Beauty' at Theatre Severn, Christmas 2013 and Meads Mini Musical,

August 2013. He has also tried his hand at presenting and has already worked for the media giants BBC and Channel 4 and has performed at Blue Chip Corporate events in some of the most prestigious venues around the country.

Josh supports many charities:
- Bobby Moore Cancer Charity
- St Francis Hospice, Essex
- Little Havens Hospice, Essex
- Essex Air Ambulance
- St Luke's Hospice, Basildon

He performed at a Eurovision reunion event in aid of the Toma Fund, also participated in Celebrity Dance with James and Ola Jordan from the popular BBC1 'Strictly Come Dancing' in aid of Essex Air Ambulance.

His off-stage interests centre on music and has a large collection of instruments from baby-grand piano to guitar and he is currently writing many of his own songs.

Josh's father Richard a builder by trade has been managing him along with agent Anne Sullivan, wife of Gary Sullivan the founder of Stage Ability. Richard says that he thought the building trade was daunting and unpredictable but the entertainment world is more so.

His latest Video 'Game Over' is out and proves that with his voice and personality he will be in great demand and he still lives in Laindon.

True to his word Josh made a special appearance at St Luke's Hospice Annual Thanks Giving service held at the Basildon College Sports Centre on the 7th June 2015 to celebrate their 25 year anniversary and he sang "The impossible Dream".

Josh has recently changed his stage name to Josh James and in December 2015 he will be appearing at Shrewsbury Theatre Severn where he plays Dick in the pantomime 'Dick Whittington'.

His main aim still is to give endless joy to millions of children – and their parents.

Figure 37 Josh on Fenchurch Station with my grandchildren - Photograph by Ken Porter.

Josh has now emigrated to Canada to try his luck there.

Ernest Longstaffe-B.B.C. Producer and Composer

Ernest was born at Newport, Essex, in 1884; son of Edgar Longstaffe the famous Victorian artist, he was living with the family at Hill View, Basildon Rise, Laindon at the time of the of the 1901 census, his occupation at the time being an Auctioneers Clerk.

Like his father he was very talented but his talent was theatrical. Unlike today though there were no television talent shows that could project you into the limelight, you had to start at the very bottom of the profession.

Ernest did and one of his first jobs was to post bills for 'Karno'. Fred Karno was the inventor of slapstick and impresario. He transformed the music hall by creating a riot of laughter out of chaos, originating the custard pie in the face.

Being around the theatre world obviously inspired Ernest, he could sing, danced and had learnt to play the harmonium but he would do whatever was required of him to progress his theatrical career.

On the 30th May 1908 he married Emma Hodge at St Mary's Church

Figure 38 Ernest Longstaffe - third from the left

Kilburn. At the time of the marriage he was still living in Laindon and Emma doesn't appear to be working but by the time of the 1911 census they are both in Blackpool performing at one of the piers variety shows and lodging with one of the pier attendants. Ernest's occupation is given as Musician and Emma as an actress. Emma was born in St Andrews, Fifeshire.

The early years of the 1920's saw the formation of the British Broadcasting Company and their first home was Savoy Hill, off the Strand in central London. Ernest was becoming very versatile, he was turning his hand to writing, composing, lyric-writing, orchestrating, producing and conducting. This talent was just what the BBC was looking for and he was going to stay with them until he retired in 1949 at the age of 65.

The number of revues, pantomimes and variety broadcasts which his creative hand was involved in was considerable. The first being *'The BeeBee Cabaret'* in 1926, many more in the hallmark of early broadcasting of light hearted entertainment were to follow: *'The Advanced Sparks'*, *'Micromatics'*, *'The rush hour'* and *'The Saturday Game'*. It was not long before he became best known as a variety producer with shows such as *'Palace of Varieties'*, *'The Old Pig and Whistle'* and *'Happidome'*.

On the 24th January 1935 the BBC broadcast *'Our Town'* which was written by L du Garde Peach, the composer was Ernest, it was produced by Ernest and he conducted the Revue Chorus and Orchestra

He was also well known for some of his foot-tapping ballads, such as:

'When the Sergeant Major's on Parade' published 1925. *'Where's the sergeant'* published 1938. *'The leader of the town brass band'* published 1929. *'The Captain of the fire brigade'* published 1933. *'Archie of the Royal Air Force'* published 1928. He wrote the words and music for all these. It appears that he had a thing about men in uniforms but there were many others, how about *'The little grey church on the hill'* published in 1924, I wonder if it was St Nicholas Church, Laindon that inspired him on this occasion.

"Far, far away in the home-land, a quaint little church I can see:
On a hill through a field looking over the weald, and I hear its bells calling to me.
Though it's a memory, only a dream, often so near me they seem.
Little grey church on the hill, your sweet bells are chiming "Ding dong!
Won't you come home, come home?"
Even in dreams I can still hear that message rhyming "Ding dong!
Why do you roam, why roam?"
Don't you know that fond hearts anxiously are yearning for the day they'll see their wanderer returning?
Dear ones whose love keeps the old home fires ever burning. Ding dong!
Won't you come home, come home?
When shall I see it? Well may be though fortune's not easy to gain, still there should come a day not so far, far away when the bells needn't call me in vain.
Then for a journey, no matter how long, homing for life's evensong.
Little grey church on the hill, your sweet bells are chiming "Ding dong! Won't you come home, come home?"
Even in dreams I can still hear that message rhyming "Ding dong!
Why do you roam, why roam?"
Don't you know that fond hearts anxiously are yearning for the day they'll see their wanderer returning?
Dear ones whose love keeps the old fires ever burning. Ding dong!
Won't you come home, come home? Home, come home? Come home?

In addition to the other song titles he composed a number of musical monologues, such as: *'Confidence'* and *'Kisses'* and was involved in stage works like the musical comedy *'His Girl'* and the revue *'Up with the Lark'*.

In 1943 the BBC Variety department was evacuated to Bangor, North Wales. They took over a large mansion house with performers living in rented accommodation around the town. Ernest went with his orchestra and performed at the County Theatre. At the time he was playing more classical music than the other orchestras that were also evacuated, so his guests tended to be more upmarket such as Harriet Cohen, a classical pianist. On another occasion Betty Driver was the guest artist and she sang *'My Devotion'*. Betty was the Betty the barmaid in Coronation Street.

On leaving the BBC in 1949 he was still full of life and continued to produce and conduct on his own. He died at the Middlesex Hospital, St Marylebone on the 23rd November 1958 at the age of 74.

Obituary – Glasgow Herald – 24 November 1958

Mr Ernest Longstaffe, former B.B.C. producer, who gave listeners such programmes as "Palace of Varietries", "Happidrome" and "The Old Pig and Whistle" died yesterday in Middlesex Hospital. He was 74.

When he retired in 1949 to produce theatrical shows, Mr Longstaffe had been a author, composer and conductor, as well as producer, during his 23 years with the B.B.C. He was a variety producer for the past 14 years.

Mr Longstaffe began in the theatrical business the hard way. At one time he posted show bills for Karno, played the harmonium and danced and sang in chorus of comic operas. Many radio stars owed their start on the air to him.

John Georgiadis...........Conductor and Violinist

For those who enjoy good music I recommend that you pay a visit to the delightful and musical website **www.johngeorgiadis.com** to read about John Georgiadis, a talented violinist both in orchestras and as a virtuoso soloist and recording artist, conductor and all round musicologist.

John Georgiadis, is a thoroughly Essex man, he was born in Rochford Hospital in 1939 and he moved with his family to a house called 'Cranleigh' Dunton Road, Laindon in 1951. His time in Laindon was to be some of the most influential years of his early life, those in which the pattern of his life's work were set out for him, although he had moved to Paris to study in 1960. As he has said, his Laindon years, were "the years that I 'kicked off' the strict control

Figure 39 John Georgiadis

that my father had previously exerted over me and that subsequently led to my having some success as a violinist."

John's modesty conceals the fact that his career as lead violinist of some of the UK's leading orchestras (at the age of 23 he was principal violinist in the Birmingham Symphony and of the LSO at 26) together with his world-wide conducting activity has, because of his work with and on behalf of music in Essex, particularly with the Youth Orchestra, led to him being granted in July 1990 the Honorary Degree of Doctor of the University of Essex.

Much of the detail of John's musical career is set out on the website to which readers are thoroughly recommended. As it reveals, John came to live in Laindon when his father Alec, needing a venue to set up his business which was involved with rabbit pelts, obtained the house named "Cranleigh" in Dunton Road, Laindon, the former residence of the Buckenham family. With its capacious outbuildings this proved ideal for what was needed and Alec Georgiadis was soon producing the Cranleigh Cleaning Cloth, a process which involved him taking on members of the local community, mostly female, as operatives.

Alec Georgiadis (Alec's father was Greek) was an amateur violinist and he was keen that his son, John, should also master the instrument. His ambition was such that he laid down what appeared to some of his employees to be some pretty hard and fast rules concerning just how long and hard son John should practice the violin daily. It was not unusual to hear remarks about "poor John" being locked in the bathroom until all his allotted exercises had been completed.

It was while John and his family were living at "Cranleigh" that chance was to play an important part in influencing John's development as a violinist. Alec Georgiadis and John's mother, Pat, were on a walking tour in the Austrian Alps when they were intrigued to hear the sound of a violin being played with considerable panache coming from a mountain hut.

John's parents sat outside the log cabin and were treated to an impromptu recital for over an hour and, when the violinist responsible eventually emerged and his unseen audience had applauded the artist, it turned out that the instrumentalist was no less than the renowned Willi Boskovsky. Concert master of the Vienna Philharmonic Orchestra for forty-three years. Boskovsky was the instigator of the Vienna New Year's Day

Figure 40 John is on the left playing the violin. By kind permission of John Peters

Concert that, principally devoted to the works of the Straus family, can still be enjoyed every year at Christmastide on BBC television.

With their shared interest in the violin Boskovsky and John's parents stood chatting for some time at the end of which they offered that almost obligatory and polite invitation to Boskovsky, that so often happens in such holiday encounters between strangers who never expect to meet again, to give them a ring any time he was in London. Much to the surprise of John's parents, Willi Boskovsky, in London on an engagement and staying at the Savoy Hotel, gave them a ring and as John says, he must have experienced "a serious shock" when they arrived at the hotel in his dad's work van! He was probably even more surprised when, no doubt anticipating being entertained by some wealthy English family at their country estate, he discovered that on arrival at Laindon, he was expected to spend his visit performing with, coaching and advising both his teenage host and John's father in a musical weekend.

Not having anticipated a "working" weekend, Willi Boskovsky had not brought his own instrument with him, but to his great credit and John's lasting and deep impression, he borrowed Alec's violin manufactured in 1924 and got down to it. It must have been something that very few people in Laindon would ever have expected to hear outside one of the great London concert halls. It certainly was for John, in particular, an incredible and thoroughly motivating experience that was to set him firmly on the worthwhile path of the admirable career he has pursued ever since.

By the time John arrived in Laindon he was already attending the Royal Liberty School in Romford before moving onto the Royal Academy of Music. He finished his studies at the Royal of Academy in July 1960 at the age of 21 when he learned that he was to be given the Countess of Munster Award of £350 to enable him to study in Paris for a year under the celebrated Professor Bernadetti.

This was not his only award as the media press reported that: "On Saturday Mr Georgiadis shared with another musician the Queen's Prize, top award in the Royal College of Music competition open to cellists and violinists. The adjudicator was world-famous violinist Yehudi Menuhin.

During his 10 years at the Royal Academy of Music, Mr Georgiadis proved himself a brilliant pupil and later he learned that he was to receive the coveted Dove Prize, awarded by the Academy only for great merit.

He also received an Academy award for a violin recital before he took up his studies in Paris he will spend three weeks in Bayreuth, Germany, leading the Students' Orchestra in a series of concerts and recitals.

While all this was going on he still found time to get engaged to Miss Susan Salter of Neath, Glamorgan who had also been studying at the Royal College of Music as a viola player.

In the previous twelve months John had won the Gulbenkian Commonwealth award of £100 in the Festival of Commonwealth Youth concert in London and following this, the Royal Overseas League Music Circle invited him to play in a concert before the Queen Mother on the 20th June 1960. He has also performed before the Queen.

Although he did not spend a considerable amount of time in Laindon, his first professional engagement was in fact for the Laindon and District Operatic Society for which he received ten shillings for his week's performance at Laindon High Road School, performing Gilbert & Sullivan's 'Patience'. He also gave a recital, sponsored by Basildon Civic Arts Society at

Timberlog County Secondary School.

At the age of 23 he commenced a two and half year period as leader of the City of Birmingham Symphony Orchestra and in 1965 and 1979 he had two spells as the Leader of the London Symphony Orchestra (LSO).

He then went on to spend eight years of conducting studies with legendary Roumanian conductor, Sergie Celibidache. This led him to travelling the world as a guest conductor to many orchestras.

- 1982-1984 Music Director of Bristol Sinfonia
- 1986-1990 Leader of the Gabriele String Quartet (1st Violin)
- 1989-1992 Director of Orchestral Studies at the Royal Academy of Music.
- 1991-1992 Principal Guest Conductor of the Queensland Symphony Orchestra
- 1994-1996 Music Director of Bangkok Symphony Orchestra. (BSO)
- 1972 to present Co-Founder and Music Director of the London Virtuosi Chambers Orchestra.
- Royal Philharmonic Orchestra, which he conducted at the Barbican.
- Guest of the Sultan of Oman.
- Conductor of the Essex Youth Orchestra for more than a decade.
- 1996 – With the BSO he was Guest of King Sihanouk of Cambodia.

In 1972 he was made a 'Fellow of the Royal Academy of Music' (FRAM) and in 1976 he was made 'Fellow of the Guildhall School of Music'.

For 18 years he was involved in working with young people, coaching and conducting all over the world, including the European and Chinese Youth Orchestras. He was also Principal Conductor of the Essex Youth Orchestra for more than a decade (1980-1991) and he also has become a prolific recording artist on various labels and several of his CDs have received the highest accolades.

He has recorded as a: Conductor, Director, Solo Violinist, Orchestral soloist and chamber music player. Below are some of his Solo Violinist recordings:
- Elgar Salon Music
- Viennese Gems
- Moeran, Rhapsody No2
- Bax Berkeley Bridge
- The London Virtuosi – Volume 1/ 2/3/4
- Sibelius String Quartet

When he manages to get away from his music, he loves a game of golf and likes messing around on the computer. He currently lives with his wife and three children on the East Coast of England.

Greg Smith... Producer

I wonder how many of you remember the hugely successful Confessions series of films for Columbia Pictures:
Confessions of a Window Cleaner.
Confessions of a Pop Performer.
Confessions from a Holiday Camp.
Confessions of a Driving Instructor.

If so did you know that the producer Greg Smith was a Laindon boy, although born in Twickenham in 1939 he was bought up by his Aunt in Laindon from an early age after his parents died.

Greg Smith:

Figure 41 Greg Smith

Brian Cordell commenting on the Laindon & District Community Archive web site remembers that he had a drop handle bar push bike, a lot of hair and a saddle bag on his bike which always looked like it was stuffed with books. Another comment by Colin Pegrum confirms that he lived in Elizabeth Drive with Mrs Smith who he understood was his mother but as we now know was probably his Aunt. With the Basildon Development moving the family they moved first to a bungalow in Waverley Road then later to St David's Road, Langdon Hills.

He went to Laindon High Road School and became Head Boy. His initial drama experience was with the Youth Drama Group that operated out of the Laindon Community Centre. In 1955 the Group changed its name to Community Drama Club (C.D.C.) and its first performance at the New Hall in 1959 was 'Sailor Beware' and in it was Greg, he appeared in a number of drama plays during the 1950s, another being 'Ring for Cathy'.

He went to a drama school in London and on leaving at the age of 15 he joined the Argyle Theatre Touring Company. It was in 1958 while he was travelling back and forth to Fenchurch Street, London on the Laindon line that he was involved in the Dagenham Train Crash on the night of 30 January 1958.

Jean Pattle a friend was waiting on Fenchurch Street Station to catch the 6.35 train with a group of friends when she realised the early train had not gone, so shouting to her friends she jumped in the last carriage, just before the train pulled out.

Jean report in an article on the Laindon & District Community Archive site informs us that the 6.35 which her friends were on ran into the back of her train. She was trapped for some time and appears to have passed out. The following are her words:

'I heard a voice call my name and realised it was my friends I had left at Fenchurch Station, they were looking for me. They had been on the 6:35 which had run into us but thankfully they were unhurt. One of the boys Greg Smith stayed with me all the time it took for the firemen to get me free, then one fireman carried me in his arms with my badly broken back, up the steep embankment at the side of the track and laid me on the ground'.

He took a job as a runner to impresario Bernard Delfont and later he worked as a theatrical agent with Billy Marsh and MCA (Music Corporation of America). This organisation closed in 1964 so at the young age of 25 he established his own talent agency in London's Golden Square and assembled a respectable client list of producers, directors and writers including the Irish-born film maker Norman Cohen.

Greg and Norman set up Prophet Enterprises and together they made the documentaries, "Brendan Behan's Dublin" and "The London nobody knows".

The film 'The London nobody knows' shocked film audiences with flat capped James Mason exploring the seedy streets of post war London and poverty. It initially went out as a support film to the movie version of 'Till Death Us Do Part' (1965).

Television sitcoms being transferred to the Cinema in the 1970s was becoming big business, resulting in Greg and Norman acquiring the rights to Dad's Army for Columbia Pictures with the film version being released in 1971. This was soon followed by the film based on Spike Milligan's novel "Adolf Hitler – My Part in His Downfall" for United Artists. Our Greg was on his way and with the relaxation of censorship for broader comedies he teamed up with the director, Val Guest for the first Confessions film.

Greg in 2001 said: "I don't think British sex films were ever really sexy, they were risqué but that's how British people liked it. All I wanted to do was to make people laugh. I didn't want to push things for the sake of it but I think the censor was in a state of shock!'

While all this was going on Greg married Cheryl Cocklin who was later to become Michael Barrymore's wife. Greg went on to marry Lynda Bellingham (The OXO mum) and this what she had to say on their first meet: *'My first husband, Greg Smith, a struggling young film producer, entered my life when he came to dinner party at my flat. He was cocky and flash with an eye for the ladies but also charming and bright. He was about to make a film called Confessions of a Window Cleaner, a more risqué take on the Carry On style and I suggested for the lead role an actor called Robin Askwith, whom I'd seen in a kit kat advert.'*

Greg and Lynda married in 1975 and they held their reception in Stage 7 at Elstree studios where they were making the film 'Confessions of a Driving Instructor' and Windsor Davies and George Layton attended but it only lasted a year. Greg went on to marry Valerie Van Ost who was also an actress and she worked as a casting director on two of his films in the early 1980s – 'The Boys in Blue' (1982) and 'Funny Money' (1983).

Greg always believed that one of his greatest successes was co-producing "Buddy – The Buddy Holly Story" with Laurie Mansfield and Paul Elliott. It opened at the Victoria Palace Theatre, London in 1989. It moved to the Strand Theatre in 1995 and after 13 years it left the West End for UK and European tours. It won many awards.

In 1998 he produced the film 'Animal Farm' in a production studio he set up in the Luggala Valley, Wicklow Mountains, Ireland. He used live animals and animatronic doubles.

The following are a few more of his other credits:
- Never Too Young to Rock (1975) – Musical film starring Glitter Band.
- The Importance of Being Dublin (1975) – Documentary
- Stand up, Virgin Soldiers (1977) starring Robin Askwith and his wife Lynda Bellingham
- Remake of 'The 39 Steps' (1978) starring Robert Powell, John Mills
- Night Nurse (1978)
- David Copperfield (1999)

Moving to Television he produced:
- The Shillingbury Blowers (1980)
- Rude Health (1989) – Channel 4 sitcom
- Great Expectations (1989)
- Magwitch – starring Anthony Hopkins which received four Emmy

nominations.
- Othello for the BBC

Back to the stage:
- Royal Opera House production of 'Porgy and Bess' (1993)
- Musical 'Jolson' with Brian Conley in the title role (1996)
- Great Balls of Fire (1999)
- Animal Crackers
- Zipp (2003)

In the early 2000's we find Greg involved romantically with Shirley Bassey but again the relationship did not last and it is understood that Shirley was devastated over the split, she believed they were destined to end their days together. It is understood a heart attack and work load put pay to the relationship.

Finally just before he died on 19 February 2009 he married for the fourth time to Gloria Thomas.

One obituary said: 'It is my sad duty to announce that my friend and Sex Comedy Legend, Greg Smith has died at the age of 69.

Greg spent the majority of his years working out of Elstree Studio and reporter Paul Burton shortly after his death suggested to them it would be good to see a stage, a room or an area of the studios named after him-has it happen?

Graham Kendrick...Father of modern worship music.

"Shine Jesus Shine" This well-known hymn was written by 'Graham Kendrick' who was born on the 2 August 1950, at Blisworth Northamptonshire where his father Reverend Maurice D Kendrick became pastor of the small village chapel.

After several happy years at Blisworth the family in May 1957 moved to Langdon Hills where the Reverend Kendrick, became the new pastor of Laindon Baptist Church in Langdon Hills. They moved into the 'Revesby' a newly-decorated manse in the High Road. As you would expect he joined the Baptist Choir. It was however through his mother that his Christian faith was forged through her reading bedtime stories which had woven into them stories of forgiveness of sins and becoming Christian.

It was a particularly turbulent time for the church and the community as a whole as the New Town of Basildon was just starting to be developed and the quiet town of Laindon and Langdon Hills was beginning to feel its impact.

The family were to stay six years, during this time he went to Langdon Hills Junior School. However a further call meant that his father became the minister of Putney Baptist Church, Putney and though Graham was still only thirteen he had already started to show signs of his musical talent that was going to make him one of the most prolific of British Christian singer-songwriter and worship leaders and who was later described as a 'father of modern worship music'.

Figure 42 Graham Kendrick

While in Putney Graham attended the local comprehensive school and later trained as a teacher. In an interview for the Cross Rhythms magazine in 1990 he said that while attending the comprehensive school *'the only other Christian I knew in the whole school was my brother, so that tested the reality of my faith – this was in the sixties and everybody was getting into all the 60s hedonism and whatever. And that challenged me – 'what am I going to do, how am I going to live my life?' But we survived and I think it actually strengthened my faith to be in that testing situation.'*

He had learnt to play the guitar and so decided to delay taking a job as a teacher and form a small band with Simon Dennis called 'Parchment'. But his career really took off when he formed a Christian beat group 'Whispers of Truth' which comprised of his brother, sister and a few friends. It was a time when Christians were starting to use the pop music of the day to communicate their faith in Christian coffee bars which were normally decorated church halls.

Figure 43 Laindon Baptist Church, Langdon Hills. Ken Porter's photograph.'

Although he had trained as a teacher he could see his diary filling up so he decided to take a year out to see where it led him. He soon met up with Simon Dennis who also sang and played guitar. Graham bought an old Ford Escort van and somebody gave them a PA system and they were on their way calling themselves 'Parchment'.

For a time he worked as a solo concert performer and recording artist. He also became associated with the organisation Musical Gospel Outreach, recording several albums. His first being 'Footsteps on the Sea' released in 1972. Then in the late 1970s he teamed with Geoff Shean and Kingway Music to produce an album of worship songs he had written.

Kendrick then for a time worked with Rev'd Clive Calver's groundbreaking mission team as a member of "In the Name Of Jesus". Calver went on to run British Youth for Christ and the Evangelical Alliance before leaving the UK for America. Graham however, has remained faithfully to the UK Church.

In 1989 he released a single 'Let the Flame Burn Brighter' which reached number 55 in the UK Singles Chart.

In 1995 he was awarded the 'Dove Award' which is an accolade by the Gospel Music Association of the United States to recognise outstanding achievement in the Christian music industry. The awards were established in 1969 and represent a variety of musical styles, including rock, pop, hip hop, country and urban.

The Brunel University in 2000 awarded Graham an honorary Doctorate in Divinity (DD) in recognition of his contribution to the worship of the Church. This was followed in 2008 by a second 'DD' from Wycliffe College in Toronto, Canada.

One of his greatest achievements was the formation in London in 1987 of the 'March for Jesus'. It began as a City March and it emerged from the friendship of three church groups, led by Gerald Coates, Roger Foster and Lynn Green along with Graham. The movement over the next three years spread across the UK, Europe and North America and finally across the world with hundreds of smaller marches emerging in its wake.

In 1994 the first Global March for Jesus covered every time zone and involved over ten million Christians from over 170 nations. It is estimated that, by the final Global March for Jesus on 10 June 2000, over 60 million people in 180 nations had taken part in the March for Jesus.

Although the founding organisation disbanded after the 2000 march, March for Jesus continues in many countries in multiple and varied initiatives. In the USA, Jesus Day is the day that many thousands of people gather to pray and march in the name of Jesus.

Graham is a member of the Charity 'Compassion' which encourages audiences worldwide to understand worship as a way of life. It operates in over 24 countries and facilitates the support of over a million children.

Although based in the UK, in fact he lives in Croydon with his family, he still travels internationally participating in tours, festivals, conferences and training events as worship leader, speaker and performer. It is no wonder he has been described as 'The Father of Modern Worship Music.'

Graham has had his critics, Quentin Letts has described him as King of the happy-clappy banalities" and "the nations eminent churner-outer of evangelical bilge" but fellow songwriter and former band member with Graham, Stuart Townend says "I have no doubt that in 100 years' time the name of Kendrick will be alongside Watts and Wesley in the list of the UK's greatest hymn writers.

Some of his well-known songs:
- 'Shine, Jesus Shine'
- 'Knowing You'
- 'Amazing Love'
- 'The Servant King (From Heaven You Came)'
- 'Meekness and Majesty'
- 'God with Us'

- 'O Lord, Your Tenderness'
- 'He That Is In Us'
- 'Go Forth In his Name'
- 'Lead me to the Cross'
- 'History Makers'
- 'For This Purpose'

Richard George Tovey .... *Actor*

Richard was born on the 14 November 1981 at Billericay to Carole Haynes and George Tovey, he has one older brother Daniel. Although he was brought up in Billericay he attended Harold Court Primary School, Romford and then Shenfield High School. His parents run a coach transfer business between Essex and Gatwick Airport, 'The Gatwick Flyer'.

Figure 44 By kind permission of charity 'breakthrough breast cancer'

As a young lad he had one of the highest 1Q's for his age and though he was very interested in archaeology and museums which his parents supported and encouraged him in taking him to digs and they even bought him a metal detector. He was however easily bored and often found himself in trouble at school. At one point though he wanted to be a history teacher but he says that after seeing such films as 'Stand by me', 'Dead Poets Society' and 'The Goonies' he decided he wanted to be an actor.

He soon became a child actor with his first part in his last year at Junior School being an extra in The Bill. He played the part of a traveller who shouted "Oi" and threw a football at a police officer. Not much but he was making money, his parents however warned him about showing off and not to boast.

As Richard says: most of his school friends then came from fairly wealthy parents so nobody seemed to take any notice.

He had joined a local drama club where he was spotted by a talent agent. He work very hard and missed a lot of schooling which worried his father but his mother convinced him to let Richard continue and in 1994 at the age of thirteen he was cast in 'Mud' a children's TV series broadcast on CBBC.

Mud was about a group of children from a London Tower Block on holiday to an outdoor activity centre called Felfront Heights along with their social worker. The series initially was about their adventures around the centre but when they returned the following year it had closed down so they found themselves with the social worker in the local village, this led to getting involved in witch finding and time travel. Playing opposite him was Russell Brand, Brooke Kinsella and a teddy bear called Steve.

By now he was working regularly in professional productions and when he left school at 16, he enrolled for BTEC in performing arts at Barking and Dagenham College and while there he worked part time as a kitchen assistant at the King's Head pub, Billericay. He only lasted a year, being expelled for refusing a role in the school play 'Rent' in favour of a paying acting roll in a commercial for McDonald's. The college said, if you take this we're not going to invite you back and if you leave you will never work again. Obviously Richard knew his own mind and was confident in his own ability, he left and now this college cites him as one of its famous former students.

It was in his early twenties when he really began to make his name with Alan Bennett's play 'The History Boys' at the Royal National Theatre. Where he was given the part of 'Rudge' a plain speaking, sporty type. He toured Broadway, Sydney, Wellington and Hong Kong. He also played the role in the radio and film adaption. However he suffered badly with spotted skin and decided to quit the production as it was affecting him psychologically even though they plastered him with plenty of makeup. Even today he controls his skin problem with medication.

He was a little insecure because he was now finding that he had not spent the same amount of time at drama schools like many of his peers, so he enrolled in numerous workshops and readings offered by the National Theatre.

His list of credits in Theatre, Television, Radio and films is unbelievable and I am not sure what is considered his most famous part because there have been so many. Such as: The Pirates! In an Adventure with Scientists (2012), Doctor Who (2 Episodes), Voyage of the Dammed, Were wolf George Sands in the drama Being Human, played Henry Knight in the episode 'The Hounds of

Baskerville', lead role in the ITV sitcom 'The Job Lot.' In 2014 he was appearing at the Royal Court Theatre, London as Jason in 'The Pass'. Gavin and Stacey (4 episodes). In 2015 in the film Banished he plays the character, James Freeman and is currently appearing in the American TV series 'Looking'.

On top of all that he has written three plays, although not yet performed and has had a short story published in the women's magazine Company. In 2012 he won the Royal Television Society, UK Best Comedy Performance with Sarah Solemni in 'Him & Her', also SFX Awards, UK won their 2011 Cult Hero award in Being Human.

I wonder how many people in the Borough realised that he was a Billericay cum Basildon Boy with nearly 100 credits to his name and he is only in his early thirties.

Lee Martin Evans.............................Comedian

I have to admit I knew very little about Lee Evans but after looking him up on Wikipedia all I could say was, Wow! Wow! Wow! - What a staggering career and though he was born in Avonmouth, Bristol on 25 February 1964 he spent his late childhood and early teenage years in Billericay.

The family actually moved to Billericay when he was eleven, where he enrolled at Billericay School. It is reported that he was a victim of bullying possibly why he took up boxing.

After Billericay School he spent two years at Thurrock Art College he then followed his father into the entertainment world. His father at the time was a nightclub performer.

In his later teenage years he moved to Scarborough, Yorkshire and joined a punk rock group as a drummer – 'The Anonymous Five'. However it was his comedy act that shot him into the limelight. His act was so energetic that he perspired to such an extent that he used to take a break during performances, shower and change before returning to finish his act and after a few performances he would throw his suits away because the drycleaners refused to handle them. He often used a dysfunctional character called Malcolm to illustrate unusual characters.

Figure 45 Lee Evans

He created the character on a man he saw cleaning the floor with a v-mop at a service station.

He married Heather Nudds on 22 September 1984, both 20 at the time and their daughter Mollie was born in December 1993.

His first major break came at the Edinburgh Festival in 1988 prior to that he had spent four years touring the working men's clubs, followed by five years on the alternative circuit.

In November 2005 he performed in front of 10,108 people at the Manchester Arena a World Record at the time for a solo comedy act. Then in 2008 his stand up touring act called "Big" he performed in front of over 500,000 people covering 59 dates. He released in November 2008 a DVD, filmed while he was performing at the O2 arena, it sold well over 1,000,000.

In 2011 he toured the UK again and his new act was called "Roadrunner". Due to popular demand he increased the number of dates over 14 cities to 67. This was followed up in 2014 with his 'Monsters' tour where he was on stage 65 times but none of these compared to his 1996 tour, 'Different Planet Tour' with 114 shows.

If this was not enough he appeared in many films:
- Mouse Hunt
- There's Something about Mary
- The Fifth Element
- Funny Bones
- The Ladies Man
- The Martins
- The Medallion
- Undertaking Betty
- Freeze Frame

He provided voice overs for Zippo in the TV series 'Diotopia' and Train in the film 'Magic Roundabout'

As you would expect he appeared on TV. Channel 4 late night show 'Viva Cabaret, both as a host and guest performer and a Channel 4 series 'The World of Lee Evans'. His talents did not finish as he co-wrote and starred in the sitcom 'So What Now' for the BBC. In May 2007 he starred in the television adaption of the book 'The History of Mr Polly'. He also appeared in the 2009 Easter special of Doctor Who, the 'Planet of the Dead'. We must not forget his theatre work, In 2004 at the Albery Theatre, London he played the crippled servant Hamm in Michael Gambon's 'Endgame', then between September 2013 and January 2014 he starred in the play 'Barking in Essex' at London's Wyndham's Theatre.

Not only was he a Comedian, Actor, writer, he could also sing, play the guitar, bass guitar, electronic keyboard, piano, mandolin, ukulele and drums, now that is what you call an all-round entertainer.

Interesting snippets;

- He shares the same birthday with his namesake, sprinter Lee Evans who won the 400 metres at the Mexico Olympics
- His nickname was Monkey Boy.
- In 1993 at the Edinburgh Festival he won the Perrier Comedy Award
- Was awarded an Honorary Doctorate from Anglia Ruskin University in 2009
- Second Doctorate from the University of East London in 2010
- Honorary Fellow of the Welsh College of Music and Drama – his father Dave Evans is Welsh.
- He has his own production company, 'Little Mo Films' that produces his stand up DVDs.
- In 2010 he ran the London Marathon (4 hours 55 minutes, 10 seconds)

In 1997 he moved back to Billericay as he had previously been living down the road in Westcliff-on-Sea. Then in November 2014 came his shock announcement on the Jonathan Ross Show that he was going to retire from stand-up comedy so that he could spend more time with his wife Heather and daughter Mollie.

In trying to explain his thinking to Jonathan Ross, he said: "I started off cleaning toilets when I was a kid and I've had loads of jobs and I just kept working and working and working and my dad always said to us 'you've got to work' so I've just continuously worked, done comedy, toured, but I've ignored, I think for far too long, my missus and I want to spend a lot more time with her."

As you can imagine social media went wild:
- Well I am absolutely devastated – Lee Evans best comedian in the World.
- Glad I got to see Lee Evans before he quit
- I am gutted that Lee Evans is retiring, my favourite comedian of all time

- I give him 12 months before he launches a 'return' tour and acting jobs in between.

The following comment was from someone who was not so keen on his comedy but was taking by his acting:

'But I saw him in the lead role of the film "History of Mr Polly" and I thought he was great in it. I much preferred him playing the part to John Mills in the old film. Lee was quite charming in it and I think he brought some of his own natural humour to the role in a most appealing manner. His ordinariness was not boring but in this case, most attractive and touching.'

There is no doubt he had his critics but one cannot argue about his massive talent, it must have been the Billericay air.

Ireen Sheer............................Singer/Actress

Ireen nearly slipped through our fingers but that is understandable as she has really made her name in Germany where she is affectionately known as 'The Gala Queen'. However she was born in the registration district of Romford on the 25 February 1949, Irene Margaret Wooldridge. Her parents were Ronald and Erika Wooldridge, (nee Mirwaldt) and they were married in June 1947, her mother being German.

Her home town in her formative years was Billericay and she lived in Bellevue Road. She went to the local Billericay School and is probably the most internationally famous luminary from the school. Her musical talent soon shone through and at the tender age of 12 she won a talent competition organised by the BBC singing the Elvis Presley song 'It's Now or Never'.

She received drama and singing lessons but after school got a job as a bank clerk but in 1966 she decided to enter for the Basildon Carnival Queen Contest and won.

Figure 46 Ireen centre. By kind permission of Basildon Carnival Association.

However, her real ambition was to get into musical comedy so after initially training she started singing with various bands, in-particular 'The Family Dogs'. She had changed her name to Ireen Sheer as she felt it sounded better than Irene Wooldridge. Then in 1970 she started her solo career. As her mother was German, Ireen as you would expect was bilingual and in 1971 she released her first song in German "On Holiday". In 1973 she released "Goodbye Mama" and it reached number 5 in the German Charts. Also in 1973 she found herself starring in the film "If every day were a Sunday".

Many of her following records became hits and she began appearing as a guest on several different television music shows, including several appearances on the ZDF Hit Parade, one of Germany's most popular music programmes.

Then in 1974 she represented Luxembourg in the Eurovision Song Contest. She came 4th with *Bye Bye, I love you*. Four years later in 1978 she appeared for Germany in the contest, this time coming 6th with the song *Fire*. She was back again for Luxembourg in 1985 singing alongside Annemieke Verdoorn, Franck Olivier, Chris Roberts, Diane Solomon and Malcolm Roberts, reaching 13th with the song *Children, Kinder, Enfants*. She made two other attempts with Germany to get into the Song Contest but did not progress beyond the German preliminaries.

Ireen married singer Gavin du Porter in 1976 and though they sung several duets together it was not a happy marriage and after 24 years they were divorced, then in 2010 she married her second husband Klaus-Jurgen Kahl. She says she would have liked to have had children during her 30s but by the time Klaus came into her life she was too old.

In between all this she went on to have several more hits with titles such as *Xanadu, A Kiss from you, Tennessee Waltz* plus many more, there were also albums. She has also sung duets with Cliff Richard.

As one would expect she has received a number of awards along with several golden records during her glittering career of nearly fifty years. She has twice received the highly-prestigious German music award *Golden Tuning Fork* (1981 and 1993) plus *Golden Microphone, Golden Europa* and the *Silver Otto*.

In February 2012 she released her latest album "Brighter than the stars" and she is still going strong and charming both her gala audiences and fans with numerous appearances. To appreciate how good she is I suggest you listen to her on You Tube and you will soon realise what a professional she is and although she performs in Germany, she is still a Billericay, Basildon Girl.

Figure 47 Basildon Recorder

Graham Arthur Ernest George Bradly (Bonney)..........................Basildon's First Pop Star

By the end of the 1950s Basildon New Town's population was approaching 40,000. The Town Centre, Housing Estates, Industrial Estate were all beginning to take shape but there was still no Hospital, Police or Fire stations, post office or railway station and the social life was a little thin on the ground. But it did have the Locarno (Mecca) which later became known as Raquel's nightclub a scene of an early Depeche Mode concert. It was here that produced Basildon's first pop star Graham Bonney.

I am personally not a great favourite of Facebook but I have to admit sometimes it comes up with some real gems and Graham produced one of them on 27th August 2015.

Figure 48 Graham and his first Ukulele age 6. By kind permission of Graham Bonney

'Hi everybody – it's me, Graham Bonney (Bradly...without an ("e")! I lived at 50 Beeleigh East, Basildon. Went to Fryerns Technical Grammar School. Was born in London, 5 White Road, Stratford E15 on 2 June 1943. Then moved to Basildon in 1954. In the Espresso Five was: Lead singer, Pete Cackett, later known as PYE recording artist Becket Brown. Drummer, Tom Berry, who is still my best friend today. Lead guitarist Colin Hill, bass guitarist, Roy Sullivan, who later joined Chris Andrews, with whom I just did a big show in Switzerland last weekend. Any more information, I am glad to oblige! I am still "a rocking"! Love to Basildon! Regards Graham Bonney.

And true to his word Graham spoke to me over the telephone from Germany a few days later and filled in a lot of his early life and how he got into music.

Graham was born in Stratford on the 2 June 1943 to Beatrice and Arthur Bradly (Unfortunately he did not get on with his father), his grandparents also lived nearby in the street. His first school was Bridge Road infant's school but he soon moved to West Ham Church School which was near to West Ham Church of 'All Saints' where he was also a choir boy. The School dates back to 1723 and it was here where he passed the eleven plus and went on to Stratford Grammar. The nearest sports facilities was Wanstead Flats so sporting activity at the school was low on the agenda. Graham hated his time at the school and as he says why do you want to learn Latin unless you want to be a doctor and he can remember standing in the bath on a Friday night looking at all the marks from either the cane or ruler.

The family moved to Basildon in 1955 and Basildon's first Grammar school 'Fryerns Grammar and Technical' was still being built so for a year he had to get up at 5.30/6am spend 45 minutes to 1 hour travelling by bus then have a mile walk to Hornchurch Grammar School.

Prior to this at the age of four he decided to join a local dance club his

Figure 49 Espresso Five, Locarno, Basildon 1962. By kind permission of Graham Bonney

sister, Heather, belonged to. Anything his Heather did he wanted to do, they later moved to another dance school in the Canning Town area. He liked it there, there were 250 girls and about four boys. I wonder why? But it was hard work, Wednesday and all day Saturday. Although by the time he was at Stratford Grammar School he kept it quiet from his friends as he realised that in those days he would have been called a cissy.

Entertainment must have been in his blood as he started to abscond from school, going up town to audition for parts in films. His first small part was being in a crowd in the film 'The Pool of London' and later 'Mandy' featuring Jack Hawkins and Jane Asher, the film was released in 1950 so Graham would have been seven years old. In 1954 he got another small part in the film 'Divided Heart' this was soon followed with his biggest part to date in the musical comedy film starring John Mills 'It's great to be Young'. He spent three weeks learning a dance routine at Elstree Studios and all the time the school believed he was off sick, on this occasion he claimed to be down with pneumonia. His father used to drive him in his car with Graham lying on the floor in the back of the car to London Bridge Tube station where he would be picked up, though for a time he stayed with a friend in London.

Then as mentioned in 1955 due to the upholstery firm his father worked for moving to Basildon, Graham's days of becoming a film star ceased. To Graham, Basildon was paradise, they had moved with his Grandparents from a very deprived area not much more than a slum, playing in bombed out building sites etc to a newly built 4 Bedroom House, number 50 Beeleigh East.

Although he had to give up his dancing and small film parts this was compensated by the countryside all around them. His mother loved the garden and like the neighbours tended them with a passion. However he is not so impressed with the area today when he takes a wander down memory lane. The Town Centre was still to be built.

When Fryerns finally opened about a year after the family moved down he got a transfer. Although he had passed the eleven plus, he had missed a lot of schooling because of his other activities so the school decided to place him in the class of students that had just passed the thirteen plus. This did not disturb him because it meant that he was always amongst the oldest children in the school and had no prefects to badger them.

Unlike the other schools he enjoyed his time at Fryerns, there was the playing field and he found himself in the Rugby Team 1st eleven, captained the schools Tennis Team and later played football at right wing for Craylands Youth Team. At last he felt like a lot of other kids who had moved from the East End to Basildon that there was some hope for them.

It was also around this time that Rock & Roll had hit the music scene and bands were popping up everywhere. One day in the changing room he came across Ken Williams who also a very good footballer playing an electric Guitar. He decided there and then he wanted one, with the dance/show group back in Stratford he had been playing the ukulele, often earning thirty shillings a night (£1.50p) so he thought that the guitar would not be too difficult. His mother had taken a job as a waitress at the Jolly Friar pub so with her extra money bought him an electric guitar and amplifier. So with Ken they formed a small school band and playing at the school, though he admits he was not very good, but it was a start.

Graham eventually left school with a string of 'O' Levels and got an apprentice job with Marconi's with day release at Thurrock College but his heart was now in music. There was a local lad Peter Cackett slightly older than him a singer whom he admired from a distance. He decided one day to knock on his door to see if he would join his band he was trying to form and after attending one of the group's practices he decided to.

They initially named the band 'Pete and The Black Jacks' but this only lasted for a few months before they changed to Espresso Five, the year was 1961. Graham to this day does not know where they got the name from. However, their reputation in the Basildon, Laindon, Thurrock, Castle Point area gradually grew and they found themselves practicing and playing in many venues around the area, such as the 'The Century' Pitsea cinema, Craylands Youth Centre, Kingswood Community Centre, Laindon High Road School Youth Centre on a Friday night, this is where I first came across them. Eventually they became the resident Basildon band at the Locarno Mecca in 1961.

Figure 50 Super Girl released in 1966

He went on to perform with the group called 'The Embers' performing at the Star-Club in Hamburg. In 1964 Larry Page invited Graham to become the lead guitarist with the 'The Riot Squad' but after three unsuccessful singles with Pye Records he left in 1965 to go solo. He also started writing his own songs along with Barry Mason. His first single "My Little World is Blue" was unsuccessful his second single "Super Girl" reached number 13 in the UK charts in 1966. However in Germany it reached number 1 in several of their charts and remained in the top ten for several months. It is understood it sold over a million copies and you can still hear it on YouTube today. In Germany's most popular Bravo-Music box he stopped the Beatles going to number one with 'Yellow Submarine'. Although 'Super Girl' was his only success in Britain his fame grew in Germany and between 1966 and 1973 he had 14 singles in their top 50 and all of them going into the Top Ten. He also appeared in several TV shows – 'Beat Club', 'Hits a Go Go' and others. In 1967 and 1968 he won Bravo Otto award as top singer and toured with the Beach Boys. Then in 1969 he returned to England to co-host early editions of the TV show 'Lift Off'.

Since the middle of the 1970s he has been one of the most booked entertainers in Germany with up to 200 live shows a year and because he had British citizenship it allowed him in the early days to perform in both East and West Germany. The East German audience loved him. In fact he performed all over Europe and made many TV appearances, Netherlands, Belgium, Austria, Switzerland, Italy and Spain. Eventually after many years jetting back and forth he eventually relocated to Cologne.

Figure 51 Graham Bonney in 1966

The Girl with LA-LA-La', 'Hey Little Lady', 'Brandy' and Papa Joe are just some of his hits. We must not forget that he is also an excellent guitar-player.

In 2005 he released the long player "DER LETZTE ROCK 'N ROLL" with English and German songs and in the summer of 2006 he made a new recording of Super Girl, exactly 40 years after the first.

He has over the years toured with many famous groups such as the Beach Boys and has become a close friend of Ireen Sheer our Billericay girl, who you would also have read became a big German star.

From an early age flying had always intrigued him, resulting in him eventually owning and flying his own aircraft PA 28 Piper Cherokee and flying back and forth to Germany. He obtained his pilot's licence in the early 1970s at the London School of Flying at Elstreet Airport.

He married his second wife a German Stewardess Iris in 1984 and they live in the country just outside Cologne where he has his own studio and garden. He often pops back to England where his children from his first marriage still live nearby in the Chelmsford area. It also allows him to keep in touch with his some of his old colleagues from the Espresso Five days.

Depeche Mode..................Greatest Electronic Band

Depeche Mode, where do we start, if there is any person or group of people that have firmly placed Basildon in the minds of the world it is Depeche Mode an electronic band formed in 1980. Q Magazine said they are "the most popular electronic band the world has ever known" they also included them on their list of "50 bands that changed the world".

Figure 52 Plaque in James Hornsby School – Ken Porter's photograph

The Sunday Telegraph referred to them as "one of the greatest British pop groups of all time". Fans from all over the world come to Basildon to visit where they lived and special tours are arranged to take them around.

Well who are they, the current members are Andy Fletcher, Martin Gore and Dave Gahan and previous members have been Vince Clarke and Alan Wilder. There has also been touring members Christian Eigner and Peter Gordeno.

In the early days of Basildon many new churches were springing up as the population grew. One such church was St Paul's Methodist Church in Ballard's Walk, Lee Chapel North and in 1968 this was going to be the place that several of the Depeche Mode artistes were to meet.

Vince Clarke

Vince was born Vincent John Martin on 3 July 1960 in South Woodford, moving with his parents in 1965 to a four bedroom Corporation House in Shepeshall, close to Falstones at southern end of Lee Chapel North. He went to

Bluehouse Infants School (now Phoenix), then on to Laindon High Road Secondary Modern School.

At about the age of nine he joined the 5th Basildon Boys Brigade juniors

Figure 53 5th Basildon Boys brigade with Vince in the third row second from right and Fletch in the front row. By kind permission of Steve Burton

which was attached to the Methodist Church (St Pauls in Ballards Walk). The Brigade met at Janet Duke Infants School and it was here that he was to meet and befriend Andy Fletcher.

Vince started writing songs at the age of 15 and was to become the founder of Depeche Mode. Being a member of the Boys Brigade he had to go to church and like others he became a Christian and it was not long before he started to go to the church Youth fellowship events, where he would meet other future members of Depeche Mode. The Captain in the photograph has now turned 80 and still occasional plays the organ on a Sunday Morning at the Church.

Vince began to learn to play the violin and later went on to learn to play the guitar, bass guitar, piano, mandolin, melodica, keyboards and synthesizers. He left Laindon High Road School in 1976 with five 'O' levels and continued his education at Basildon College.

Music was obviously in his blood and he formed or was involved with a number of bands before Depeche Mode came on the scene. In the late 1970s he formed a band 'No Romance in China' then in 1979 with Robert Marlow and Martin Gore formed 'French Look' followed by 'Composition of Sound'. In 1980 Dave Gahan joined as singer, previously Clarke had provided the vocals, it was then or shortly afterwards they changed the name to 'Depeche Mode' the name of a musical magazine. At roughly the same time they moved away from guitars for synthesizers. Again at the same time he adopted the stage name of Vince Clarke. Now we had the four originals Vince Clarke, Andy Fletcher, Martin Gore and Dave Gahan.

Vince stayed with them for two years but decided to leave because he felt the group musically were going in a different direction than he wanted to go. However it was not long before he teamed up with another school mate Alison Moyet to form the popular synthpop band 'Yazoo', and their first record 'Only You' went to the top of the charts. They went on to produce two albums, 'Upstairs at Eric's' and 'You and Me Both' but unfortunately soon after the second album in 1983 they split, with Alison going to have a successful solo career. Though they did reform in 2008 for a series of live dates to celebrate 25 years since their split. In the U.S. the band was known as 'Yaz'.

Vince did not stand still and he soon teamed up with Eric Radcliff and formed a new band called 'The Assembly' and with singer Feargal Sharkey they had a top 5 hit with "Never Never". He also founded with Eric the label Reset Records. By 1985 this project also went sour but following an ad in Melody Maker for a singer he teamed up with Andy Bell and formed the group 'Erasure'. By 1989 Erasure had established themselves as one of Britain's best groups and in fact won the Brit Award for the Best British Group.

Although they became very popular in the U.K., they are also extremely popular in mainland Europe and South America and to date have sold over 25 million albums, their latest being released in September 2014, The Violet Flame. It went to number 20 giving the duo their first Top 20 album since Other People's Songs in 2003.

In between Vince has been involved in a number of other projects with various artists and in May 2009 he was awarded the "Outstanding Song Collection" prize, during the Ivor Novello Awards ceremony in recognition of 30 years in the music industry,.

Vince is married to Tracy Hurley and they have a son Oscar and they are currently living in Brooklyn, United States.

Andrew Fletcher (Fletch)

Andrew John Leonard Fletcher, affectionately known as 'Fletch' was born on 8 July 1961 in Nottingham and he moved with his family to Basildon at the age of two. They moved into Woolmer Green in the northern part of Lee Chapel North. He went to Chowdhary Infants School, which was named after local Doctor D.S. Chowdhary who had served the Laindon area for 30 years. He died in 1959 and the school opened in 1966.

Andy from a very early age was a very confident young child and amongst his peers a natural leader.

Figure 54 Fletch, Martin Gore and friend Steve Burton at a party in Lee Chapel North. By kind permission of Steve Burton.

He was to meet up with Vince Clarke at St Paul's Methodist Church and they were both heavily involved in the Methodist Boys Brigade Youth Club and later the Youth Fellowship Group. He in fact stayed in the Boys Brigade until he was 18 and during his involvement with the church, he and Vince would preach and try to convert non-believers but he is no longer a practising Christian but it remains in his blood and he often feels guilty about not going to church.

After leaving the infants school he went to St Nicholas Comprehensive School, Laindon where he eventually took 'A' Levels. He paid for his record collection with money raised from delivering copies of the Basildon Echo. After leaving school he got a job with Sun Life Insurance, London, south of the River. By now Fletch and Vince Clarke had formed a band 'No Romance in China' in which Fletch played bass guitar. Not long afterwards in 1980 Fletch met Martin Gore at the Van Gogh Pub in Paycocke Road, Basildon. The three of them formed 'Composition of Sound' which as you would have already read was the forerunner of Depeche Mode, with rehearsals often in each other's front rooms.

Fletch was not as musically talented as the others but because of his personality played a very pivotal role in the success of Depeche Mode, on many occasions handling the band's business interests such as legal and other non-musical matters.

In 2002 he launched his own record label 'Toast Hawaii' and signed the band 'CLIENT' but they left the label in 2006 and there has been no activity since. When away from the Depeche Mode scene he toured as a DJ and carried out the occasional festivals in Europe, Asia, South America, places that Depeche Mode have not visited. Also for a time during the 1990's he owned a restaurant, 'Gascogne' in St John's Wood, London.

He married his long term girlfriend Grainne Mullan in January 1991 and they have two children, Meghan and Joe.

Finally those that have seen Depeche Mode perform often wonder what Andy actually does and what actually his role is. Well it has been said that Martin Gore writes the songs, Dave Gahan sings them and Andy Fletcher shows up for photo shoots and cashes the cheques.

Martin Lee Gore

Born on the 23 July 1961 in Dagenham, but at an early age the family moved to a small terraced house in Shepeshall at the southern end of Lee Chapel North. When he was 13 he found out that his real father was an Afro-American G.I who had been stationed in Britain. He was not to meet him until he became an adult.

He went to Nicholas School where he passed 'A' levels in German and French. On leaving school he found a job with NatWest clearing house in the city. Prior to leaving school he had formed in 1977 a band that lasted for two years with class mate Phil Burdell called 'Norman & The Worms'. Their first proper gig was in the common room at Nicholas School. Around at the time was the all-girl group the 'Vandals' with Alison Moyet, Gail Forey and Sue Paget. They all knew each other at Nicholas.

Martin appears to be the only one of the future Depeche Mode group that actually played cricket for his school team.

Figure 55 *Martin playing in his house in Shepeshall. By kind permission of Steve Burton*

He knew both Andy Fletcher and Vince Clarke, through going along to the Boys Brigade and church but he maintains that he was strictly an observer.

As previously stated it was in 1980 that Martin Gore met Andy Fletcher at the Van Gogh Pub who persuaded him to team up with him and Vince Clarke and become part of the Composition of Sound band, later to become Depeche Mode. With Vince Clarke moving on in 1981, Gore took over the song writing and in recognition of his contributions to popular music, Gore received the 1999 Ivor Novello Award, given out annually by the British Academy of Songwriters, Composers and Authors.

Martin developed a love of black leather and at 18 bought his first leather jacket, he also had a habit of swapping clothes and make up with his girl-friend, though hedid not walk around dressed as a woman as suggested by the media.

During the Bosnia crisis of the mid 1990s, Martin gave a substantial donation and became a Trustee of the 'Voices of Children Foundation', charity started by the Rector of St Nicholas Church, Laindon, Naunihal Paul. A charity established for the wellbeing of the children of Bosnia. For a time during the 1990s he lived in Berry Lane, Langdon Hills.

In 2012 he linked up again with Vince Clarke and released an electronic dance album, entitled 'Ssss'.

Gore married Suzanne Boisvert, lingerie designer and model in August 1994 and has three children, Viva Lee born 1991, Ava Lee born 1995 and son Calo Leon born 2002. They divorced in 2006 and in June 2014 Gore married Kerrilee Kaski. He currently lives in Santa Barbara, California. He suffered from alcoholism for a number of years but is now sober.

In addition to his song writing and singing he played, Guitar, keyboards, synthesizer (he purchased his first at 18 for two hundred pounds), bass guitar, piano, theremin, organ, harmonium, accordion, melodica, recorder, banjo, percussion, tronichord and turntables.

Oh! He also speaks fluent German.

David Gahan (Callcott)

Figure 56 Dave Gahan

Dave as he was known was born David Callcott in Epping on the 9 May 1962 but when he was six months old his father, Len left and divorced his mum Sylvia two years later. His mother remarried to Jack Gahan. He did not meet his father again until after the death of his stepfather. His mother had moved the family to Bonnygate on the Fryerns estate, Pitsea, following the divorce.

He went to Barstable Comprehensive School, leaving in 1978 with only one 'O' Level in art. He did not enjoy school life and with his unsettled home-life led him into petty crime, resulting with him being suspended from school and ending up at juvenile court three times with a short spell in Borstal. He admits himself it was the excitement of nicking cars, spraying walls and being chased by the police. No wonder he was known as the wild one, the complete opposite to the boys from Lee Chapel North.

In a period of less than a year he went through at least twenty jobs but eventually he signed up at Southend Art College and after three years he got the British Display Society Award which enabled him to get a job doing displays in large stores.

Figure 57 The poster was designed by Vince Clarkes younger brother Rodney Martin. By kind permission of Steve Burton

Dave started to hang around and attend the gigs of Composition of Sound particularly when they were practising or performing at the Paddocks Hall in Pound Lane, Laindon. Dave at some point was approached by Vince Clarke to become the group's singer, after he had heard him perform David Bowie's "Heroes" and his debut was on the 14 June 1980 at Nicholas School, Laindon. It was soon afterwards that Dave suggested they change the name to Depeche Mode. The name was taken from a French fashion magazine. It means "fashion in a hurry". There was no specific significance to the name, other than members liked the sound of the words.

Although Dave concentrated on his singing he did write a number of songs and in 2013 with the release of their 13th Album Delta Machine he is credited with writing the songs 'Broken', 'Secret to the End' and 'Should be Higher'.

In 2003 he released his first solo album, 'Paper Monster' which he co-wrote with guitarist friend Knox Chandler. This was followed by the Paper Monster tour that included a performance at 2003's Glastonbury Festival.

Unfortunately Dave found his way into drugs but he is however now considered a recovering drug addict. He suffered a minor heart attack while performing in New Orleans in 1993. In August 1995 he attempted suicide and the following May overdosed. This was followed in 2009 when he fell ill in Greece and subsequent tests revealed a malignant tumour in his bladder. At various other times he has suffered from a torn calf muscle and strained vocal cords. Saying all that, he is still performing with Depeche Mode and others.

He has been married three times, his first marriage was to Joanne Fox with whom he had a son. His second marriage was to Teresa Conroy, a former Depeche Mode publicist. He is currently married to Jennifer Sklias and they live in New York City with their daughter and Jennifer's son from a previous relationship, who Dave officially adopted in 2010.

Alan Charles Wilder

Alan answered an advertisement placed in the music magazine Melody Maker by Depeche Mode following the departure of Vince Clarke. They were looking for a Keyboard player and someone aged 21 but Alan was 22 but he lied about his age. He initially joined as a tour keyboardist in January 1982 but soon became a full member of the band.

Unlike the rest of the band Alan did not come from Basildon, he was born on the 1 June 1959 and bought up in a comfortable family environment in Acton, West London. He went to St Clement Dane's Grammar School in Hammersmith, but was not very interested in schooling only really interested in music and languages. With the encouragement of his parents he started to learn the piano at the age of eight and later learned the flute at St Clement Danes. He became a leading musician in his school bands.

He left school during the sixth form and went on the dole but after a little persuasion from his parents he contacted various recording studios and eventually got a job at DJM studios in New Oxford Street. Not much of a job but after the various bands had finished in the studios he had the opportunity to play around on the keyboards and drums.

Figure 58 Alan Wilder

He became friendly with a group called 'The Dragons' joined them and moved to Bristol, after two years and fed up he returned and got involved with a number of groups before answering the advert in the Melody Maker.

After thirteen years with the band and partly due to increased tension within the group he announced his intention to leave on the 1 June 1995 on his

36th birthday. On leaving he decided to concentrate on the musical project he had created in 1986 called 'Recoil'. He did however reunite with Depeche Mode Teenage Cancer Trust concert at the Royal Albert Hall on 17 February 2010 and received a rapturous reception.

Wilder currently lives near Horsham, West Sussex with his Norwegian partner, they have a daughter born in 2011 and he has two further children from a previous relationship.

Depeche Mode

The above are the main players of the band over the last thirty five years and if you want to know more about these individuals and the part they played in the massive success of the group I suggest you read the book by Simon Spence 'Just Can't Get Enough' the title taken from their single of the same name released in October 1981. It peaked at number 8 in the UK Charts, top 20 in Sweden and number 4 in Australia and was making waves in other countries. It was the third of their singles, their second single 'New Life' reached number 11 in the UK charts and got them a spot on Top of the Pops, but 'Just Can't Get Enough' got them on the 1981 Christmas show of Top of the Pops.

By now the band was enjoying live dates in Amsterdam, Brussels, Hamburg and Paris the music world could not get enough of them.

To date Depeche Mode have had fifty songs in the UK Singles Chart, thirteen top 10 albums in the UK charts, two of which went straight to number one and they have sold over 100 million records worldwide. This has been made up of 13 studio albums, ten compilation albums, six live albums, eight box sets, 13 video albums, 70 music videos and 53 singles. This has made them one of the most commercially successful electronic bands the world has known.

The band's album 'Songs of Faith and Devotion' hit No.1 in the UK and USA simultaneously, making them one of only eleven UK Acts to do so. The others being The Beatles, Led Zeppelin, Rod Stewart, Pink Floyd, John Lennon, Phil Collins, Radiohead, Coldplay, Susan Boyle and Adele.

As you can imagine they have released too many albums, been on too many world tours and too many UK gigs to list them but although they take a break every now and again they are still going strong. For example they toured North America from 22 August to 8 October 2013 with their latest Album 'Delta Machine'. Then they toured Europe with the tour ending on the 7 March 2014, at Olimpiski in Moscow.

They were awarded the 'Best International Group-Rock/Pop' in March 2014 at the ECHO Awards in Germany.

Finally fans from all over the world flood to Basildon and go on the tours organised by Bas Productions (www.basproductions.co.uk). They have been running tours for four years, the last two in June 2015 and no doubt they will organise tours for 2016. Visitors are guided by friends and associates of the band from their early days in Basildon. The tour normally takes about three hours visiting the key sites of the bands development, from childhood homes and locations around the town where they practiced and performed.

Although the group are now flung far and wide I still believe they see Old Basildon as their home. Is it not time the council found a way to honour them. For example there is a bar in Tallinn, Estonia dedicated to them and in March each year in Moscow fans march in celebration of Dave Gahan's birthday.

Just as a point of interest there is a road in Basildon 'The Gore', please do not be mistaken as being named after Martin Gore, it is in fact named after a farm that used to be in Rochford Hundred. The farm was mentioned in the Court Rolls in 1374.

Chapter 4 - Politics

Charles Edward Leatherland - Lord Leatherland of Dunton

Charles Edward Leatherland purchased the Old Rectory in Dunton in 1934. The property consisted of six bedrooms, attached stables and twenty acres of land and a moat. He kept two or three horses and was an enthusiastic rider and supporter of the Dunton Hunt.

Figure 59 Lord Leatherland

Leatherland was not an original Essex Man; he was born in Birmingham on the 18th April 1898 to John and Elizabeth.

John at the time of the 1901 census was a gardener at St Andrews Church of Wales, Dynas Powis, Glamorganshire and they were residing in the Truant School Lodge and Elizabeth was the Lodge Keeper.

They moved back to Birmingham in 1902 and this is where he was brought up. Charles with his three younger brothers went to the local elementary school Harborne. He was a bright boy and won essay prizes run by the Birmingham Evening Post. To help his parents out he took a paper round earning half a crown a week, then at 11 years of age he worked as a boot boy for a local JP. His role included cleaning half a dozen pairs of shoes, a dozen knives, forks and spoons, collecting coal, stoking the furnace and grooming a large dog before setting off to school two miles away by 9am. He had similar function in the evening and at weekends he had to roll the lawn to get ready for tennis and clean at least twenty windows.

Charles mother died in 1908 when he was 10. His father later married their housekeeper, Rose. John was now working as a Valet for a wealthy solicitor in Edgbaston. In 1917 he joined the firm Cadburys and stayed there until he retired in the 1930s, he then moved south to live with Charles until he died in 1945. These were humble origins for someone who was to become a very respectable Labour Peer.

Charles was always very conscious of only having a very basic education but before he left school he taught himself shorthand and typing which stood him in good stead for a life in journalism. His first job after leaving school was as a shorthand typist in the office of a golfing magazine. Then he joined Birmingham Council as a clerk typist. Unfortunately he did not get on that well with his stepmother so he left home and went into lodgings.

At the age of sixteen Charles lied about his age and he enrolled in the Warwickshire regiment. By the time he was 18 he was a Company Sergeant Major in a machine-gun battalion seeing service in France, Belgium and Germany.

Unfortunately as the result of wounds, he had a limp for the rest of his life. On one occasion during a meeting of Labour Peers he reminded them that his limp was as a result of action. 'Don't forget, I saw service on the Somme'. Douglas Houghton, Lord Houghton of Sowerby retorted with 'Ah yes, Charlie, you may have been at the Somme but you were not at Passchendale as I was'. An unforgettable moment of humour for those that were there!

On the first day following his demobilization he joined the Labour party and for this reason he wrote in the Daily Herald in 1949:

"I remember standing in front of a coal cart in Birmingham Bull Ring one Sunday night in February 1919. It was the day after I left the army. One of my worlds - the world of the war - had just ended. Another was just beginning. I was a little nervous of this new world. It all seemed so strange. There were no signposts to show which way to go. I listened to the man on the coal cart who was speaking. He was thinking of this new world too. He was saying how it could be a better world, a happier world, a healthier world. I joined the Labour Party before the meeting ended. I had been a good solider. I wanted to become a good citizen. I felt that in joining the Labour Party I had become one."

In 1921 he began his career as a journalist working for the Macclesfield Courier, where he rose to become Chief reporter and sub-editor and as one would expect moved to Macclesfield where he rented a council house. Then in 1922 he married Mollie Morgan and a year later they had their first child, Irene.

In 1923 and 1924 he won gold medals in an international essay writing competition, with the medals being presented by the Prince of Wales of which he was very proud.

In 1924 the family moved to London and rented a house in Clapham where he joined the Labour Party Press department in London writing party pamphlets, speaker's notes for MPs and reporting on what happened in the House of Commons as a lobby correspondent.

The family kept moving, first to Hooking Green in Harrow then in 1928 to Westcliff- on-Sea where his son John was born. Job change again when he joined the Daily Herald in 1929 as political sub-editor, became Assistant News Editor in 1938 and finally News Editor in 1941.

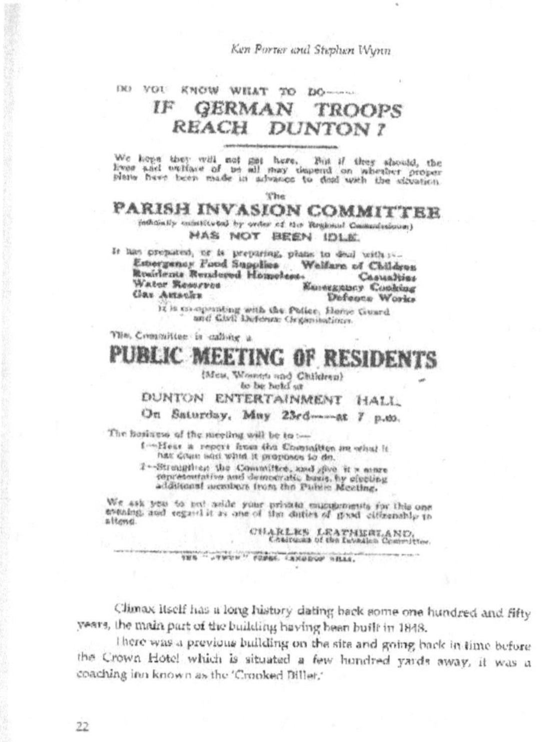
Ken Porter and Stephen Wynn

DO YOU KNOW WHAT TO DO——

IF GERMAN TROOPS REACH DUNTON?

We hope they will not get here. But if they should, the lives and welfare of us all may depend on whether proper plans have been made in advance to deal with the situation.

The

PARISH INVASION COMMITTEE

(officially constituted by order of the Regional Commissioner)

HAS NOT BEEN IDLE.

It has prepared, or is preparing, plans to deal with:—

Emergency Food Supplies — Welfare of Children
Residents Rendered Homeless — Casualties
Water Reserves — Emergency Cooking
Gas Attacks — Defence Works

It is co-operating with the Police, Home Guard and Civil Defence Organisations.

The Committee is calling a

PUBLIC MEETING OF RESIDENTS

(Men, Women and Children)
to be held at

DUNTON ENTERTAINMENT HALL

On Saturday, May 23rd——at 7 p.m.

The business of the meeting will be to:—

1—Hear a report from the Committee on what it has done and what it proposes to do.

2—Strengthen the Committee, and give it a more representative and democratic basis, by electing additional members from the Public Meeting.

We ask you to put aside your private engagements for this one evening, and regard it as one of the duties of good citizenship to attend.

CHARLES LEATHERLAND,
Chairman of the Invasion Committee.

Climax itself has a long history dating back some one hundred and fifty years, the main part of the building having been built in 1848.

There was a previous building on the site and going back in time before the Crown Hotel which is situated a few hundred yards away, it was a coaching inn known as the 'Crooked Billet.'

22

Figure 60 Ken Porter's collection

In 1934 he then moved again this time to Old Rectory, Dunton, Essex where he and the family would live for the next seventeen years. It was here where he got involved with the local community and became a leading figure in the political and social life of the county.

During the Second World War was Chairman of the 'Dunton Parish Invasion Committee' which reported to a central Laindon group which in turn reported to a wider group based on the Billericay area. He was also Chairman of the Dunton Entertainment Committee.

After spells as a local councillor for Laindon, Dunton and Little Burstead he became an alderman on the Essex County Council and a member of the Council for 22 years and

Chairman in 1960-61.
- Chairman of the Eastern Regional Council of the Labour Party for 15 years
- Magistrate for 26 years
- Member of the Basildon Development Corporation
- Served with the Essex Territorial Army Associations
- Became Deputy Lieutenant of Essex

Unfortunately, his wife's health was causing some concern so on the advice of her doctor they reluctantly moved in 1951 to a smaller more manageable house in Buckhurst Hill. Like many of his family they would have preferred to have remained in Dunton where he more or less had become known as the local squire. Also in 1951 he was awarded the OBE for political and public service.

He believed that one of his greatest achievements was the role he played in the establishment of the University of Essex, where he was awarded an honorary doctorate in 1971. He passionately believed that education was the key to a fuller life. Having missed out himself he wanted it for others. It was also partly due to his influence and political guile that kept Buckhurst Hill from becoming part of the Greater London Council.

Figure 61 Dunton Rectory. By kind permission of Basildon Heritage

Surprisingly he never became an MP, the reason being is that he was asked in the 1940s to stand for Parliament but it would have meant financial and career sacrifices so he declined. His later life as a Lord confirmed that he would have made a very good MP. He was still attending the House of Lords at the age of 92.

It was Harold Wilson who gave him his life peerage in 1964 for his exceptional career in Journalism, politics and public service. He died in Epping 18th December 1992.

Angela Evans Smith..................Baroness Smith of Basildon

In her maiden speech in the House of Lords Angela Smith told the house: 'When I was introduced to your Lordships House, I did so as the first Baroness of Basildon – possibly the first time that a modern new town has been recognised in this way, but I have to confess to your Lordship that I am not the first Lady Basildon. The first was created in 1895 by the great Irish Oscar Wilde in his play 'An ideal Husband' which was first performed at the Haymarket Theatre."

"Lady Basildon was described as being of 'exquisite fragility' – an attribute which I doubt has ever been used to describe me but showed an interest in politics, of a kind."

When she first heard that she was going to become Baroness Smith

Figure 62 Angela Smith

she joked about being known as *"Lady Ange from Vange"* She was elected unopposed by her party colleagues and attends the Shadow Cabinet as part of her role.

Angela was born 7 January 1959, in Hackney to Emily Evans and Pat Smith but the family moved to Pitsea when she was young where she went to Pitsea Junior School then Chalvedon Comprehensive. At school she threw herself into Charity Work and fund raising committees and could often be found on the street corner with her charity tin. She also worked for a time in the Charity Shop. Other child pastimes being the Brownies and Swimming.

On leaving school she went to Leicester Polytechnic and studied Public Administration gaining a BA. In 1978 she married Nigel Smith who had been her history teacher, he was already actively involved in Basildon local politics and was a County Councillor.

Angela first started out as a trainee accountant with the London

Borough of Newham before moving on to work for the League against Cruel Sports (1983-1995), becoming head of Political and Public Relations.

Her first attempt of becoming an MP was when she stood for Southend East in 1987 but it was a decade later when she was elected as Labour MP for Basildon in 1997. A position she held until May 2010 when she was defeated by Stephen Metcalfe.

Angela was soon in the thick of parliamentary life when she introduced a private members bill to minimise waste generation and successfully managed the bill through Parliament to it becoming the Waste Minimisation Act 1998. Her abilities must have been recognised because the following positions rapidly followed.

- Government Whip, 1999
- Parliamentary Under Secretary of State for Northern Ireland, 2002.
- Department for Communities and Local Government, with responsibility for the fire service 2006.
- Parliamentary Private Secretary to Prime Minister Gordon Brown, 2007. Entitling her to attend Cabinet meetings. Appointed Privy Council.
- Enter the government at Cabinet Level Office at Minister of State level, 2007
- Minister for the Third Sector (Volunteer)

When she took up the post of Minister for the Third Sector this is what Stephan Brown, senior public affairs officer had to say: *"Prime Minister choose people to be their private secretaries who they trust implicitly and take advice from."*

The only blip on her service to the country was during the expensive scandal when she had to repay wrongly claimed expensive of £1,429. To her defence it is understood her expense claims because of her hectic work load were completed on her behalf.

Following her defeat by Stephen Metcalfe and the defeat of the Labour party at the 2010 General Election she was created a Life Peer as Baroness Smith of Basildon by the outgoing Prime Minister George Brown. Moving on to the House of Lords has not slowed her down, to date she has spoken and asked questions on over 7,000 occasions covering a wide range of subjects.

- Road Traffic Control
- Counter Terrorism and Security Bill
- Child Sexual Abuse
- Asylum Seekers: Women
- Higher Education – Overseas Students
- Police Funding

- London, Tilbury and Southend Railway
- Immigration Etc:

We know from experience that while Angela was carrying out her parliamentary duties she did not neglect her constituents. Other than dealing with queries brought to her by her constituents she lists her interest as home affairs, animal welfare, international development, employment and youth and children's issues, including child protection. She is or has been patron of several charities, including Basildon Home Start, Basildon Women's Refuge, Basildon Age Concern, the Captive Animals Protection Society and the Burned Children's Club.

Her leisure interest when she has time included watching Coronation Street and we forgive her for that, reading political biographies and Oscar Wilde novels and plays.

She has lived in Langdon Hills for many years but also has an apartment in London in the Elephant and Castle area. Angela is still only 56 so she has many years to go to even make a greater mark on our society, we wish her all the luck.

Chapter 5 - Our Footballers

The Borough have three major non-league football sides, Basildon United, Bowers & Pitsea, who both play in the Essex Senior League and Billericay Town who play in the Isthmian League, Premier Division. Billericay won the FA Vase three times during the 1970s and is only one of two clubs to do so.

If you take a drive out on a Saturday or Sunday during the football season you will be amazed at the number of boys and girls football matches being played in the Borough, no wonder young players have made it to professional status from our Borough, such as: Michael John Kightly, Andy Barcham, Stewart Robson, Darren Caskey, Justin Edinburgh, Freddy Eastwood, James Tomkins.

Michael John Kightly.. The Ryan Giggs of Non-League Football

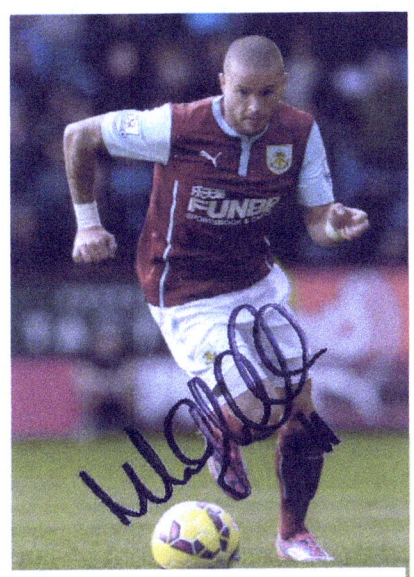

Figure 63 Michael Kightly. Ken Porter's collection

Michael was born in Basildon on the 24th January 1986 and lived in the Burnt Mills/Bowers Gifford area. He is currently playing for the Premier League side Burnley. His main playing position is right wing though he has been known to play in midfield and on the left wing.

He went to Chalveldon School and in addition to playing for the school played for Newtown and one of his earliest successes was when they beat Blackshots (Grays) in a cup final. He also played for Berry Boys football club (a Laindon club). As a school boy he was soon spotted by Tottenham Hotspur but after two years they let him go and he joined his home team, non-league Basildon United. In fact he turned up at one of their training nights and was introduced to the manager, he stayed on and had a trial that night and was immediately put in the first team for the following Saturday. But he obviously had ambitions to become a professional footballer and on the 16 December 2002 he signed a two year football scholarship with Southend United after impressing them in a five game trial period. He made eleven appearances for them before being loaned to Farnborough Town for the 2004 – 2005 season. At the end of 2005 season Southend let him go and he found himself back playing non-league football for the Conference side Grays Athletic and with them he won the FA Trophy. Comment on Facebook stated: 'He was loved at Southend we should never have let him go'.

He began the 2006/7 season with Grays but following his 10 goals by November 2006 he was spotted by scouts from the Champion side Wolverhampton Wanderers (Wolves), resulting in him joining them for a two month trail on the 17 November 2006. While at Grays he was often referred to as 'The Ryan Giggs of Non-League Football" a term I am sure he is proud of.

It was in December 2006 that he scored his first league goal in a Wolves 1-0 victory over Queens Park Rangers. This followed with him signing a two and a half year contract with them on 1 January 2007, becoming a regular first team player for the remainder of the season.

Unfortunately a play-off defeat denied them promotion to the Premier Division but he had the honour of becoming runner-up for Wolves Player of the Year 2006/7. It is also believed that around this time several clubs were keeping a close eye on him but any speculation ended when he signed a four–year deal with Wolves in June 2007.

His first full season with Wolves was hampered by various injury problems; however he signed an improved four-year deal with the club in June 2008. Wolves were promoted following the 2008/9 season and he made his first Premier League appearance at the beginning of the 2009/10 season but by September he had picked up another injury.

He then experienced sixteen months of injuries before returning to play against Newcastle United in April 2011. The beginning of the following season he found himself on loan to Watford to help gain football fitness and in the twelve games he played for them he scored three times. On his return to Wolves first team he had his longest period of Premier League football, although in fine form himself he could not stop Wolves being regulated after three years in the Premier Division. He rejected a contract extension because he wanted to stay in top flight football and he found himself joining Stoke City for an undisclosed fee on the 8 August 2012. They were probably impressed with him when he scored against them in one of his last games for Wolves. He played in 114 games for Wolves scoring 23 times.

He made an instant impact by scoring in a pre-season friendly against the German side SPVGG Greuther Furth, he followed this up by scoring in his first Premier League match for Stoke against Reading. He however fell out of favour with the Stoke manager and found himself in and out of the team. Playing in total 26 games for them but then on 2nd September 2013 he joined Burnley on loan. He went on to score five goals in thirty eight games as Burnley gained promotion to the Premier League. It was first half goals by Michael and Ashley Barnes against Wigan that secured their promotion.

Then on the 27 June 2014 he signed a three year contract and that is where he is today – Oh! He also played seven times for the England under 21's.

Andy Barcham

Figure 64 Andy Barcham-Ken Porter's collection.

In May 2013 Andy signed a three year contract with League 2 side Portsmouth, normal position left wing but has been known to play on the right and at centre forward.

Although Andy was born in Basildon on 16 December 1986 he was brought up in the Castle Point area and went to Appleton School, Benfleet. His first school however was St Margaret's, Bowers Gifford.

His footballing prowess was soon discovered and he became a full time member of the Tottenham Hotspur (Spurs) academy before signing professional in 2005. During his time with the academy he played for England under 16 on 3 occasions and with the Spurs under 18 side he was top scorer with ten goals in 22 starts. He also made 19 appearances for the reserve side but unfortunately only played once for the first team against Port Vale in the football League cup. Somewhere along the way he picked up the nickname of 'Barchy'.

In November 2007 he joined Leyton Orient (League one) on loan and he played 25 games before joining Gillingham (League two) on loan on the 25 September 2008. In his debut game against Port Vale he was named Man of the Match. This followed with him signing a six month contract in January 2009, followed up with a two year contract in the summer. He made 102 appearances for them scoring 19 goals but left when his contract expired in 2011.

By July he was back playing for League one side Scunthorpe United and signed for two years. In his first season he was the club's top goal scorer with 9 goals but in May 2013 he was released by the club following their relegation to League two. However he was soon snapped up by Portsmouth (Pompey)

He soon became a favourite of the Pompey faithful as shown when they went down 2-1 to Southend in January 2015 and he was substituted in the second half. The Pompey fans taunted the manager with 'you don't know what you're doing'. Following this substitution he had a short spell on the side lines before finding himself back in the first team but this time playing on the left side in a wing back position in a 3-5-2 system against Wycombe. A position you really need to be fit and quick, the manager was very pleased with his performance...so it's a question now of watch this space.

Darren Caskey

England Under 18 ....1 Turkey Under 18......0

DARREN CASKEY, *the captain and oldest member of the side by one month, needed the coolest of heads to secure a welcome success for England yesterday, settling a tense European Under-18 Championship final with a penalty kick 13 minutes from time.*

Responsibility fell to the Tottenham midfield player after Julian Joachim, England's most dangerous attacker, was pulled down as he tried to go past the Turkish sweeper, Serkan Recber. Expectancy weighed heavily on Caskey's shoulders in front of more than 23,000 spectators at Nottingham Forest's ground, but he had the nerve to dummy the goalkeeper before side-footing home. Thus England won this title for the ninth time, the first since 1980.

He played 6 games for the England under 18s and 9 games for the under 19. In the England Teams were Gary Neville, Sol Campbell, Paul Sholes,

Robbie Fowler and Darren also with 43 first team appearances for Spurs he was being referred to as the 'new Hoddle' but for some reason it never quite happened for him, despite his all his technical skills.

In an interview with 'The Guardian' (2 February 2015) he said 'that after I left Notts County I stuttered and stumbled a bit, not really knowing where I was going," says Caskey. "I went through several clubs and then had a lovely year in America which revitalised me. The choice was then between pottering about in the lower leagues or making a serious decision to give coaching a go. I served my apprenticeship with player-coach jobs at Kettering, Halesowen and Ilkeston. I've learned a lot that I can put into use at Gateshead and think I've still plenty to offer the game."

Being saddled with the high expectation may have been Darren's misfortune. He was born in Basildon on 21 August 1974, joining Tottenham Hotspur as a trainee, aged 16 in 1990; training alongside players like Sol Campbell, he was reckoned to be among the best of the bunch – with balance, awareness of touch and an ability to use the ball intelligently.

Figure 65 Darren Caskey

He started well with Spurs, making his debut against Arsenal in 1993 and couple of months later scored the winner against Everton. Although he made over 40 appearances for Spurs, he appeared to struggle with the club's continuous change of management and he found himself having to continue to convince them that he was worth a place, this may well have affected his form and confidence, so in 1996 he rejected a new contract and moved down a division for £700,000 to Reading.

A similar situation arose with Reading with four different management teams in as many years and although he played in 200 games for them and finished top goal scorer in the 1999/2000 season with 23 goals he only stayed on for one more season before moving to join Notts County.

He spent two and half seasons with Notts County playing in 114 games but did not appear to live up to his early reputation and in 2004 moved on to Bristol City. He did not play a game for them and he moved to Hornchurch and then Peterborough United in the same year, Bath City, Havant & Waterlooville and then Virginia (America) all in 2005.

Then there were periods with Rushden & Diamond, Kettering Town, Halesowen Town, Ilkeston Town before he joined Gateshead as player and assistant manager in 2014.

A very strange career for a man with obvious outstanding talent who kept David Beckham out of the England Youth set up. Let's hope his experience in all levels of football will let him succeed in the coaching and management arena. For a time he lived on the Heathleigh Estate in Langdon Hills.

Oh! His son Jake currently plays for Brighton and Hove.

Stewart Ian Robson (Robbo)

Figure 66 Stewart Robson

Played 8 games for the England under 21 team and made the full England squad by the time he was 19 years of age, unfortunately continuous injury was to ensure that he never played for his country at this level.

He was born in Billericay on 6 November 1964 but attended Alleyn Court Prep School, Westcliff-on-Sea and then Brentwood School. His footballing talent soon shone through and at 14 he had joined Arsenal's academy and in 1981 signed apprenticeship forms. He made his first team debut soon after his seventeenth birthday on 5 December 1981 against of all sides West Ham United who he was to later join. His usual position was midfield but could also play in defence at full or centre back.

The Times said of his debut: *'In defence no one was more impressive than Robson, a 17-year-old, playing his first league match. His tackling was crisp and clean and his covering could not be faulted'*

So there is no doubt that as a young player he showed great promise as a young footballer, both in his versatility, competitiveness, running ability and tackling.

After his debut he became a regular first team player. Arsenal Fans 1984 player of the year but in the 1985/6 season had three months out with injury and with the arrival of George Graham as manager found himself out of the Arsenal side. Resulting in him only playing five games in the 1986/7 season so in January 1987 he signed for West Ham at £700,000. He had played 186 games for Arsenal scoring 21 goals and he was still only 22 years of age.

In 1988 he was named Hammers (West Ham) Player of the Year but he was still plagued with injuries. He then lost his place following their relegation in 1989 and in the next two years only played 8 league games – in total he played only 69 times in his five years with the club so in March 1991 he signed on a free transfer with Coventry City to enable him to return to the first division. Coventry City in the following year became one of the founding clubs of newly formed FA Premier League. After playing 57 games for the club he retired in 1995 after missing the entire season through injury.

He did not stay out of football for long and he found himself joining Wimbledon first as Youth Coach, before becoming reserve team manager and finally first team coach before leaving in December 2001. Then in March 2003 he stepped in as care-taker manager for three games for Southend. In December 2004 he joined Rushden and Diamonds as Technical Director. He has also forged himself a career in the media.

He has presented on Talk Sport, Absolute Radio (Rock 'n' Roll Football), been a contributor for 'The Times' and reported for ESPN's on the 2014 FIFA World Cup. But where he has appeared to have made a considerable impact and you have to say not a very good one was with his time reporting for Arsenal TV as co-commentator. He appeared to enjoy criticising Arsenal's performances and in particular their manager 'Arsene Wenger' and because of this he found his way on to 7am kick-off, Rogues Gallery.

Although the opening paragraph of the Rogues Gallery is very critical of Robbo and his criticism of Arsenal, it also reports some of his finer moments, for example after a 4-1 defeat of Wolves a reporter had this to say about him:

'Playing with surging energy in central midfield, his efforts were reminiscent of an on-form Patrick Vieira. Several tabloids gave Robbo the perfect ten for his bewildering display, capped by an explosive 25 yard drive which tore into the net'

And though Robbo was very critical of Arsene on numerous occasions he did have this to say about him: - *"he develops players not by fantastic coaching* but by giving them the environment to express and experiment themselves. He takes the fear out of their play by coaxing them to be more elaborate, precise and imaginative." As Wenger himself sums up, "I would say that usually to win is a consequence of the quality of play you achieve."

One of the last straws for the club was when he said: 'Theo Walcott, for me, is not a good footballer. He is an athlete who puts on a pair of football boots'

This as you can imagine caused an outcry amongst the fans. It is a real shame, Robson was a really outstanding player in a difficult period of Arsenal's history and could have been a great player if it had not been for his injuries but the ubiquitous 'media career' that he has carved out has in some quarters made him very unpopular.

A final line from the Rogues Gallery: 'A sad end to what should have been a good tale'

It may be he should have followed his other talent in the less volatile world of cricket. He was a very accomplished player, playing for Coventry and North Warwickshire. It's not surprising that he also had a cricket talent, the school Alleyn Court Prep School is well known for its cricketing prowess. Denys Wilcox son of the founder of the school was not only head master but also Captain of Essex and Cambridge University and of course the legendary Essex and England all-rounder Trevor Bailey went to the school.

Justin Charles Edinburgh

Justin was born in Basildon on the 18 December 1969, however the family soon moved to Steeple, Essex where his father was pub landlord at the local Steeple pub and it was here that his interest in football started with him playing in the pub garden with his brother Jason and father Michael. In addition to playing for the local school and district he joined Maldon Saints, playing for them on the left wing.

The family then moved back to Basildon and he continued his education at Barstable School where he achieved 5 GCSE's and joined the Sunday side Beech United. One of the organisers of Beech United was Martin Fry who is currently the organist at St Nicholas Church, Laindon. He was also Justin's music teacher at Barstable but admits that Justin was not that interested in music but it was obvious to him that he had flare for football.

He was soon spotted by Charlton Athletic and spent four months training with them but it was Southend United who showed a real interest in him and he joined them as trainee, turning professional in August 1988. His first manager at Southend was Bobby Moore but it was David Webb who took over from Moore who gave him his first team debut at the age of 17. He initially played in centre midfield but as he was the only left footed player he moved to left back. He played in 47 games for them and saw them gain promotion to Division 3 before moving on to Tottenham Hotspur (Spurs).

Figure 67 Justin Edinburgh

He signed for Spurs in January 1990 for £150,000 but with the understanding that he saw the 1990 season out with Southend, joining them permanently in July. It was Terry Venables who took Justin to Spurs so it is no wonder he regards him as big influence on his career. His first game was on the 10 November against Wimbledon when he came on as substitute in a 4-2 home win. Although he was not necessarily quick he did like to come forward which gave Spurs that extra option on the wing. In 1991 he pick up a FA Cup winner's medal, team mates that day included Gary Lineker and Paul Gascoigne. The following year he married Kerri (McIntyre) and in 1993 their son Charlie was born.

In 1999 he picked up his second piece of silver when Spurs beat Leicester City in the League Cup final, although he did not finish the match as he was sent off half way through the first half because he was deemed to have retaliated against Robbie Savage. Post-match analysis showed that a late challenge on Justin and the retaliated swipe with his hand only brushed Savage's flowing locks but Savage being the prima donna he was went down like a ton of bricks.

After 236 appearances, 30 as sub, he fell out of favour when George

Graham took over and in January 2000 moved to Portsmouth on Loan and then in March transferred permanently for £175,000. In the next couple of season's he played 37 times including 1 as substitute. However by now injuries were beginning to take their toll and he did not play at all during the 2002-03 season when Portsmouth gained promotion to the Premier League and a knee injury caused him to retire at the top level.

He turned his attention to management where he joined non-league club Billericay Town as player-manager in July 2003. It was at this club that he finally retired from playing football.

He was head hunted by Fisher Athletic, joining them in January 2006 and under his management the club gained promotion to Conference South. When the Chairman left he also left by mutual consent in November 2006 joining Grays Athletic as assistant manager. Following Andy King the manager's resignation in January 2007 he became manager but a year later his contract was terminated by mutual consent.

He had a short spell at Woking as assistant manager before becoming assistant manager at the Conference National side Rushden and Diamonds in October 2008. Then in February 2009 following the resignation of the manager he took over as caretaker manager and in April of that year was appointed on a permanent basis.

It was a difficult learning curve for Justin as the club was obviously in financial difficulty but he managed to get them to finish fourth in the 2009-10 season and into the semi-final play-off against Oxford United who ran out eventual winners. In the 2010-11 season they slipped back to mid table position and in the summer of 2011 the club were expelled from the Football Conference.

The following is a statement from the Conference Board giving its reasons: *"Based on information provided by the club, it is clear that it has significant financial problems.*

The Board has no confidence in the club's ability to pay its creditors or as to its ongoing viability or its ability to meet its obligations in the forthcoming season, and in order to preserve the integrity of the competition it was with regret that the board considered it had no alternative but to expel Rushden & Diamonds FC."

Justin was out of a job yet again but it was not long before he was approached by Newport County and was appointed their manager in October 2011. The team at the time was in 23rd position in the Conference National League. He managed to help them avoid relegation and got them to the FA Trophy final at Wembley Stadium where unfortunately they lost 2-0 to York City.

The following season he led them to the play-off final against Wrexham at Wembley Stadium which they won 2-0, resulting in Newport County returning to the Football League after a 25 year absence. Previously Justin had been named Conference manager of the month in August 2012 now he was named the Conference National Manager of the year.

There were several approaches from other clubs but he stayed with Newport and guided them to 14th place in League Two for the 2013-14 season. He was happy at Newport and said in an interview with the Daily Mail Online: *"This is a brilliant club and a well-supported one. The people I work for are understanding and we have a great relationship."*

Then on 7 February 2015 with Newport County in 6th place in League Two he was appointed manager of League One Club Gillingham following the sacking of Peter Taylor. Gillingham at the time were languishing at the bottom of League One only just above the regulation zone. Justin managed to guide them out of trouble with them finishing in 12th position.

In an interview with South Wales Argus, Justin had this to say: *"I know I can't please everybody and I know there are some Newport fans who are unhappy with my decision and I can understand that." "It has been an unbelievable time in the club's history and I enjoyed every minute of it. We were trying to constantly drive the club forward and it became very personal to me." "But in any walk of life, in any job whatever your profession is, you want to strive to do your best you can, no one looks to remain at the same level, If I was that way, I would never have left the Ryman Premier League."*

A few more snippets:

In 2008 he was the new face of Nourkrin Man – a natural hair nutrition programme – preventing thinning of the hair and this is what he had to say: *"Since using Nourkrin Man I feel much more confident about my hair and I can now present on TV safe in the knowledge there are no thinning areas that the camera can pick up on."*

He has two nicknames: (1) 'Rickaaaay' due to his likeness to Ricky Butcher in the BBC TV's Eastenders and (2) 'Musselburgh' because the Scottish town "Just in Edinburgh".

He is the boss of two Toni and Guy hair salons in Essex and travels daily from Essex to Gillingham during the season.

Well our Justin is still only 46 so it's a matter of watch this space, Premier League management cannot be far away.

Freddy Eastwood .... Southend Legend

Figure 68 Freddy Eastwood. Ken Porter's collection

Following two spells at Southend plus a period as a youth player you can understand that when he finally left Southend in May 2014 a club statement said that Eastwood was a 'Southend Legend'.

Freddy was our loveable Gipsy, he was born to a Romany Family in Epsom, Surrey on the 29 October 1983. He is currently living on a small Gipsy site at Cranfield Close, Wickford (Just off the A127). He appealed to the British Government in 2006 to keep his home on the traveller's site after Basildon Council refused planning permission and in a statement to the inspector he said: *"We are Romany Gipsies and part of a small community of EnglishRomany Gipsies living along Cranfield Park Avenue!"* The government upheld his appeal saying that he was free to stay for at least the next five years. However in early 2007 Basildon Council appealed and the decision was overturned but as far as we know Freddy is still living there with his wife Debbie, daughter Chardonnay and son Freddy junior.

During his playing career with Southend he was often seen exercising his horse in the morning on the A127 near Basildon. There was the odd occasion where he committed the odd misdemeanour for example he was fined by magistrates in July 2009, after he was caught fly-tipping rubbish.

His position was that of a forward and he started with Southend Youth (1997-1999) but turned down an offer of a scholarship at Southend to join West Ham youth team, where he played alongside players of the calibre of Jermain Defoe and Anton Ferdinand. Unfortunately he was not seen to be good enough by the then West Ham manager and never managed to get a first team outing. So in 2003 he was released and considered giving up football and for a time worked as a car salesman.

But he soon joined Conference South side Grays Athletic in August 2003 and in 2003-04 season he won the Grays Golden Boot by scoring 37 league and cup goals. This also brought him to the attention of several league clubs, Swindon Town, Northampton Town, Charlton Athletic and of course Southend United.

So it was no surprise that he joined Southend in October 2004, initially on loan before joining permanently a month later. On making his debut he created an English league record for a debut by scoring the opener against top of the table Swansea City within 7.7 seconds and he went on to score another two goals in Southend's 4-2 win. He was to score two more hat-tricks for the club.

His season total of 24 goals was one of the main reasons that Southend found themselves in the League Two Play-off Final against Lincoln City at the Millennium Stadium in Cardiff in May 2005. Southend won 2-0 with Freddy scoring the first goal, resulting in promotion.

The following season was just as exciting for him as he added 23 more goals becoming Joint top scorer in League One with Billy Sharp. This helped Southend to gain promotion to the Championship division. In so doing he scored Southend's 5,000th League goal. He had really made his mark with the Southend fans.

It could not continue and although in the following season he scored his 50th goal for the club he only managed 11 in the championship and was unable to prevent Southend being relegated back after only one season. The highlight of the season though and must be one of Freddy's highlights was when he scored the only goal that knocked Manchester United out of the League Cup. A spectacular 30-yard free kick.

At 23 he was one of the most promising talents outside the Premier League and though Southend did not want him to go they were in need of funds to pay for a new 22,000-seat stadium, so in July 2007 Wolverhampton Wanderers (Wolves) stepped in with a four year deal for a move costing £1.5m.

He started well at Wolves by scoring his first goal in the League Cup against Bradford City and scoring three more in the month of August which earned him the Championship Player of the Month Award. Unfortunately in the months that followed things seem to go wrong and goals dried up and he found himself either as substitute or out of the squad so after 35 appearances which included only 10 starts he decided to leave.

In July 2008 he joined Coventry City also in the Championship division on a four year deal for £1.2m fee. He stayed to the end of his contract playing in

113 games but his goal tally was only 17. He did however score a hat-trick against Peterborough on 31 October 2009, the only player to date to score a hat-trick at the Ricoh Arena.

Just before he left Wolves he was selected to play for Wales in a friendly against New Zealand in May 2007. His eligibility came through his paternal grandmother who was born in Wales. Although he played in a crucial Euro 2008 qualifier against Czech Republic soon afterwards a back injury forced him to withdraw from the squad but he was back in August 2007 with his first international goal against Bulgaria and the manager John Toshack said: "It was a really special goal, now we have a player up front who knows his business."

It was strange that he was out of favour with Wolves but was still being selected for the national side. He scored both goals in a 2-0 win over Luxembourg but again goals dried up and in his first ten internationals he only scored four times and irrespective of what the manager had said he fell out of favour and his last match against the Republic of Ireland was in February 2011.

Just before his release from Coventry he returned on loan to Southend United and at the end of the season he had surgery on a troublesome knee problem. On 12 July he signed a two year contract with Southend.

On his return he had this to say: "I always hoped that one day I would come back and play at Roots Hall again as I had some amazing times there,"

"It has come a bit sooner than I probably thought but the club are on the brink of having some good times again, so I can't wait to help them get promoted."

"I had a really good relationship with the fans last time and hopefully I can give them something to smile about this time, so it will be a win-win situation."

While on loan he scored his first goal in a 4-0 win over Cheltenham Town and at the start of the 2013-14 season he looked as fit as he had ever been and with 4 goals in consecutive matches appeared as the manager Phil Brown said *'he was in the form of his life'*. However, he spent much of the season as a squad player, playing in 30 games, 19 as substitute and at the end of the season he was released. In 64 games second time round he had only scored 11 goals. Although he is fifth in the clubs all time goal scoring charts.

There is no doubt the fans were sorry to see him go and initially he was not sure whether to hang up his boots at 30 but in the end he did and started up his own building business.

His final words were: "*Southend will always be in my heart now though, the happiest moments of my career were all here and it's where I enjoyed myself the most*"

"*The supporters have always been superb towards me and I really hope the lads can go on one better next year and win promotion*"

As we now know Southend did and were promoted to League One after a thrilling final at Wembley where they finally won on penalties.

Southend have not heard the last of Freddy Eastwood as his young son Freddy Junior is part of Southend United Youth set up.

Steve Gary Jones

Figure 69 Steve with my grandson Kyran. By kind permission of Debbie Porter

Steve was born in Cambridge on 17 March 1970 and currently lives in Langdon Hills, where with his wife Tina in 2008 founded Langdon Pumas Youth Football Club. The club started with the under nines but within a few years they were running teams from Under 7's to under 15's. Initially they practiced at Langdon Hills Recreation ground, moving to a new facility off Dunton Road but their current home ground is at Holy Cross, Basildon.

Steve himself had started his footballing career with non-league clubs Basildon United and then Billericay Town F.C. He was at the time working in a local soap factory earning £250 per week when he was snapped up by West Ham United and earning £400 per week.

He had his first outing in a reserve fixture on 17 November 1992 against Southampton F.C. and on the 8 December 1992 made his first team debut away to A.S.Cosenza Calcio in the Anglo-Italian Cup. He scored his first goal, ten minutes into his first League one Division match against Barnsley F.C.

After three Premier League starts and five appearances as a substitute during the 1993-1994 season he joined Bournemouth and in the next couple of years he played 74 time for them scoring 25 goals. Then in January 1996 the then West Ham manager Harry Redknapp brought him back to West ham for a fee of £200,000 resulting in a further eight games.

In 1997 he moved on to Charlton Athletic for a fee of £500,000, playing 53 games for them over the next two seasons, scoring eight times. There was a short loan spell back with Bournemouth before he joined Bristol City for a fee of £425,000. During his time with them he had short loan spells with Brentford, Southend United and Wycombe Wanderers. In his time with Bristol City he played 37 matches and scored seven goals. Injury in 2001 forced him to retire from professional football and for a short time he joined Isthmian League Hornchurch F.C. as player-coach.

Figure 70 Steve with my grandson Callum. By kind permission of Debbie Porter

Since 2007 he has played the occasional game for the Rod Stewart's Celebrity Football team.

During his time with Langdon Pumas and working for Tesco at Langdon Hills, he has been taking his coaching certificates and has recently been appointed assistant manager at Burnham Ramblers who play in the Ryman Division One North League. He has stated that he is keen to move into management if the opportunity were to arise in the future. At the same time he is keeping a close eye on his son Liam who has signed for West Ham...will there be a fairy tale ending for the family?

Figure 71 Stephen Tilson

Stephen Brian Tilson

Steve a midfield player was born in Wickford on 27 July 1966 and although he played 243 games for Southend United he is better known as manager of the club.

In the seven years with the club he oversaw two

promotions and unfortunately two relegations. This spell as being in charge at the time saw him being the fifth longest serving manager in the football league.

He started his footballing career with non-league sides Basildon United, Bowers United and Witham Town before joining Southend in 1988 to 1998. He had a short loan spell in 1994 with Brentford. In his time as a player for Southend he won two consecutive promotions, scoring 26 times. In 1998 he joined non-league club Canvey Island, played in 143 games and scored 58 times, he also served as captain. He then returned to Southend in 2002 but in the next two seasons only took to the field 4 times.

While still playing for Canvey he took on a new role at Southend United as Director of the club's new centre of excellence in 1999. His responsibilities were the overseeing and developing the of club's junior teams from under 9 to 16.

His role widened in 2001 when manager David Webb departed and he took on the reserve team manager's job following the promotion of Rob Newman when he took over the first team manager's role. Steve left Canvey in May 2002 and joined Newman's backroom team on a full time basis and then in November 2003 with the club in danger of relegation from the football league he took over as full time manager. This was the start of an amazing seven years for Steve and the club as they moved from the bottom of Division Two to the Championship division until he was ceremonially put on gardening leave on 4 July 2010.

His first task was to lead Southend United, known as Shrimpers, away from the danger of relegation from League Two and this he did with four wins in his first five games as manager. One of his first successes was leading them to their first ever national Cup final in the club's history, losing to Blackpool 2 -0 in the Football League Trophy Final.

Then in the 2004/5 season along with his assistant manager Paul Brush and no additional resources he took the team to fourth place, clinching a play-off final victory against Lincoln City at the Millennium Stadium. During this period he also completed successfully the League Managers Association's (LMA) Certificate in applied management course, run in conjunction with Warwick University. Steve was voted LMA League Two Manager of the 2004/5 season.

This success was followed up the following season with Shrimpers being crowned League One Champions on 6 May 2006 and being promoted to the Championship League the second highest tier of English Football, with Steve being named LMA Manager of the Season for League One.

One of Steve's and Shrimpers memorable victories was against Manchester United on 7 November 2006 when they won 1-0 in the fourth round of the League Cup. United had 10 internationals in the side including Wayne Rooney.

Unfortunately the following season they were regulated even though they won against sides like Stoke, Sunderland, QPR, Birmingham City and Southampton. In the 2007/8 season they finished 6th, losing the play off against Doncaster Rovers. In the 2008/9 season the club held their own to finish eighth.

Then it just shows you what a precarious job being a football manager is when he was removed at the close of the 2009/10 season after they had slid back down into League Two. The club at the time was going through financial difficulties and the club's chairman Ron Martin is reported to have said that 'This has been the hardest decision during my time in football.'

He moved onto Lincoln City in October 2010 but was released on the 10 October 2011 and after a short break he joined Canvey Island as Manager but this was short lived with him being sacked after only one season. He is currently running a football academy along with former Southend United player Danny Greaves.

Following another short break we find Steve who is now living in the Benfleet area back managing C&K Basildon Ladies although he had been coaching them for several seasons. His assistant manager is Danny Greaves. Steve in an interview with the local Echo paper said; 'we have a very ambitious chairman and he wants to take the club into the top division'. The club currently plays at the Selex Sports & Leisure Club, Gardiners Way, Basildon.

James Oliver Charles Tomkins

James Oliver Charles was born on the 29 March 1989 in Basildon and was spotted by West Ham scouts playing for his local Sunday League side Holy Cross F.C. and he signed for the West Ham youth academy initially as a striker but switched at a later stage to central defence.

He went to Chalvedon School and has appeared at every youth level for England, Under 16/17/18/19/20 and under 21 making 36 appearance in all. He also featured in Team GB at the London 2012 Olympics playing in two of their matches.

Figure 72 James Tomkins

In 2005 he signed scholarship forms for West Ham and in March 2008 made his first Premier League appearance in a 1-1 draw away to Everton. Unfortunately it was his slip that allowed Yakubu Aiyegbeni to score the opening goal. Towards the end of the season following injuries to first choice centre backs he had an extended run and was voted the Young Hammer of the year for 2007/8.

Like many players he signed on in November 2008 for Derby County for a five week loan spell and made his debut in a 3-0 away defeat to Burnley. He was recalled by West Ham after playing eight times for Derby and started to feature regularly for the first-team. Though initially deputising for the injured Welsh international, James Collins he managed to stake a claim ahead of him and in April 2009 was awarded a long term contract extension.

His 2009-10 season was a little up and down though he managed to retain his place at the beginning of the season only to lose it to new signing Manuel da Costa. He regained his place and in the match against Aston villa on the 17 January he was named Man of the Match by Sky Sports.

The following season he made his 50th first team appearance against Wolverhampton Wanderers but it was the 2011-12 season that really established him as a regular first team player. He received West Ham United player of the month award for August but he was being noticed by other clubs and it looked for a time that he might sign a £4 million deal for either Queens Park Rangers or Newcastle United. In the end he signed a four and a half year deal with West Ham

He confirmed his commitment to the club by saying: *"I'm a local boy and have come through the ranks at the club and loyalty is a far bigger currency to me than money"*. He was rewarded at the end of the season for his outstanding performances by being voted by his fellow professionals into the PFA Championship Team of the Year and was also voted runner-up Hammer of the year by West Ham fans, just losing out to Mark Noble.

In the next two seasons he made 57 appearances for the first team and is currently still playing regularly for the first team having made over 180 appearances in his career to-date.

Figure 73 James Tomkins. Ken Porter's collection

He now feels that he is one of the older players and in a report in the local Echo newspaper he said: *"I feel like the older player there at the back. I have Aaron Cresswell and Carl Jenkinson either side of me and they are young lads. Time flies as it was not long ago I was the youngest player in the back-four and now I'm the oldest."* He also went on to say; *"Over the years there have been some talented centre-halves playing at West Ham which means I have some massive boots to fill."*

James has just signed a new deal with the club which will take him until 2020 at the same time he has been tipped in some quarters to be called into the first England squad of 2015. Unfortunately he suffered a broken nose in February 2015 following a clash with Manchester United striker Robin van Persie, this with injuries to his ankle and thigh had kept him out of team for several matches. However his displays have earned rave reviews from his manager Sam Allardyce, who has backed him to win an England call-up in the near future.

Chapter 6 - Other sports persons

Eamonn Martin............Athlete/Lion of Laindon

Figure 74 Eamonn Martin with his medals - Ken Porter's photograph

Michael Healy in his book 'This is Basildon' (2009) refers to Eamonn as being the 'Lion of Laindon'. Although very amused Eamonn was unaware of the accolade. After being passed many times around the hills and slopes of Langdon Hills and Dunton while training for the London Marathon, I can understand how Michael came up with the name. I am only pleased that I was always running in the opposite direction.

Eamonn was born in Bonnygate on the Fryerns estate Basildon in October 1958. He attended Manor House Junior School and Fryerns Comprehesive. He excelled in all sports being captain of the school cricket team, vice-captain of the football, rugby and athletics teams.

His first love was in fact football and he played at centre forward for the District. He also represented the school in the district sports at the longer distances, so when he became the English schools Cross Country Champion (under 15) at Swindon in 1973 he decided to make a career in athletics instead of football.

On leaving school at 16 he obtained an engineering apprenticeship with Ford Motor Company and they sent him to Barking College of Technology. On qualifying as an Engineer in 1979 he was transferred to Dunton Research where he stayed until 2001 when he moved over to Visteon. He now works for MIRA Ltd in Paycocke Road Basildon as Facility Manager, Security Controller.

On advice he joined Thurrock Harriers in 1975, however he decided that he would prefer to compete for his home town so he soon moved to Basildon Athletic Club and has stayed with them ever since and is currently

Chairman of the Club. He is also a member of the Lords' Taverners team who raise money to buy mini-buses for handicapped children and as he said in an interview that he regarded himself as the greatest fun-runner and was more than happy to run amongst other charity runners and making money for the less fortunate.

His athletic achievements are endless:
- 1973 English Schools Cross Country Champion (Junior boys) with Steve Ovett in second place.
- 1975 English Schools 1,500m Champion (intermediate)
- 1983 World Athletics Championships 5,000m semi-finalist (Helsinki)
- 1984 English National Cross County Champion
- 1984 Olympic 5000m finalist – Los Angeles
- 1985 Ran 3m 41.7 in the Essex 1500m Championship a record that still stands.
- 1988 10,000m champion in the Oslo and Zurich Grand Prix
- 1988 IAAF Grand Prix champion for the 5000m
- 1990 Commonwealth Games 10,000m Gold
- 1991 European Cup Champion 10,000m (Frankfurt)
- 1992 English National Cross Country Champion
- 1993 London Marathon Champion
- 1995 Chicago Marathon Champion
- 1999 London Marathon Masters Champion.

This is just a selected few of his amazing career events.

In so doing he represented England/Britain in:
- 3 Olympic Games, 1984, 1988 and 1992
- 2 World Athletics Championships, 1983 and 1991
- 2 Commonwealth Games, 1990

Figure 75 By kind permission of Eamonn Martin

and 1994
- 6 World Cross Country Championships

Years 1985-86 were bad years for Eamonn and were more or less written off with Achilles tendon problems and a further injury in 1987 prevented him from qualifying for the World Championships.

One of the achievements that he remembers well was winning the 10,000m in Oslo in 1988 it was the 4th fastest time in history and a new UK record which stood for 10 years, a record he was very proud of. Also top of his list are his Commonwealth 10,000m gold in 1990, winning the London Marathon in 1993 by out sprinting Mexico's Isidro Rico as he came over Westminster Bridge and the Chicago Marathon in 1995. He is still the last British male athlete to win the London Marathon but in an interview to the Mail on Line in 2013 he said: ' It doesn't give me any pride that I'm still the last British male to win the London marathon, it gives me pride that I won it on the day but to think we've not move forward in 20 years does not give me any pride at all.' He honestly believes that the attitude of to-days athletes is holding them back, they are happy to receive funding running for Britain but that's it. He doubts that they train as hard as he did.

The achievement at the time although his first Marathon and only three days after the birth of his third child, this time a boy and also named Eamonn, was not considered particularly unusual as he was the sixth British male athlete to win since its inception in 1981. There is however no doubt that his name will crop up every year until we have another British winner.

Another of his memorable experiences was beating Steve Ovett on the streets of Oslo where he was pushed to the ground after only 100 metres but he picked himself up to beat a strong field and was very pleased to have beaten such a great runner as Steve.

Some of his Personal Best times are:
- 1,500m 3m 40.54.
- 2,000m 5m 01.09.
- 3,000m 7m 40.94.
- 5,000m 13m 17.84.
- 10,000m 27m 23.06.
- 5 miles road 22m 36.
- 10K road 28m 13.
- Marathon 2hrs 10m & 50s

Figure 76 By kind permission of Eamonn Martin

Not only is he Chairman of the Basildon Athletic Club but he still trains many of the young athletes and can often been seen putting them through their paces up and down St Nicholas Church Hill.

A hill he cannot remember how many times he has run up and down it. Also since retirement he has coached and managed the England Cross Country athletes and in his spare time plays tennis as a hip resurfacing operation does not allow him to run.

On 7 January 1989 Eamonn officially opened the Markhams Chase centre where a plaque commemorating his achievements was installed. The centre is no long demolished to make way for yet another housing estate that also took away a good portion of the playing fields. I wonder where that plaque is now?

A piece on Eamonn was placed on the Laindon and District Community Archive website www.laindonhistory.org.uk and it has received the following comments:

"It is really nice to see Eamonn's photos on here. I used to go to his Basildon athletics club when I was 10 years old because I won my first open competition there. I remember one day my school teacher introduced me to him after I won my first 3 AAA championship when I was 12 years old and he signed his photo for me which I still have today. Eamonn was a person who inspired me through athletics, watching him on TV and becoming part of his club was amazing, even seeing him train. It takes a lot of dedication and I am sure he will not be forgotten for many decades to come. I wish him all the best with whatever he is doing today."
By Maria Dodsworth, was (Cain) 10/08/2014

I have no idea where the 'Lion of Laindon' nickname came from either. I will have to dig out my notes to find out where I got this from. Very amusing and interesting article!
By Michael Healy 27/01/2013

Unlike todays' athletes he worked full time throughout his career, it was not until he completed in his first Olympics that Fords became aware of the Champion they had in their midst. They did subsequently allow him to reduce his hours to help him with his training. Sponsorship was also hard to come by and his biggest pay days did not come until he won the London Marathon with prize money of £58,000 and £200,000 to compete the following year.

It's a wonder Eamonn has not as yet written a book on his life, I am sure it would make fascinating reading, just look at some of his headlines:
- Essex Champion Eamonn makes it win Double.
- Eamonn runs a fine race
- Magic Eamonn boosts Basildon to their Best.
- Martin speeds in for Essex title
- Eamonn is a runaway ace
- Martin Leads Golden Greats
- Eamonn Martin's World Shocker

Figure 77 Eamonn opening St Nicholas Church Fete. Ken Porter's photograph

- Marathon man
- The modest hero who just keeps on running

He moved to Laindon West in 1985 and then to Langdon Hills in 2003 where he still lives. Until he retired, with the arguable exception of Steve Jones,

Eamonn had been Britain's most successful distance runner since Brendan Foster's heyday in the mid-Seventies.

In September 2012 he kindly open the St Nicholas Church Bi-annual Fete, 'More than Gold'

He has had an amazing career and fully deserves the accolade 'Lion of Laindon'

Robert (Rob) Neil Denmark........................Athlete

Figure 78 Rob Denmark

Rob broke onto the national scene in 1990, he came third in the 3000 metres in the 1991 World Indoor Championships in Seville. His time was a new British Record of 7.39.55min. His main distance though was the 5,000 metres and he represented Great Britain in the 1992 Olympic Games in Barcelona coming seventh. In 1992 he set a personal best time for the 5,000 metres in the Golden Gala meeting in Rome of 13.10.24min.

1994 was however his best year winning gold in the 5,000 metres in the Commonwealth Games in Victoria, Canada against the fancied Kenyans and silver in the European Championship in Helsinki, Finland.

Unfortunately injuries brought a premature end to his career and he eventually retired from international athletics in 2002. He however did not walk away from the athletic world but took up coaching local athletes. He is affiliated to the Basildon Athletic Club, based in Gloucester Park, Basildon and coaches there alongside Eamon Martin. For many years he could be seen running around the tracts of Langdon Hills and Dunton.

In 2006 he returned to top-level athletics when he joined UK Athletics (UKA) as their talent manager. His role being to identify talent at an early age. He also works for the English Institute of Sport as a performance lifestyle Advisor at the National Performance Centre at Lee Valley Athletic centre and recently joined the likes of Steve Cram and Paula Radcliffe on the UKA endurance programme.

He was also coach to Jessica Judd, who burst on to the scene when she broke the two minute barrier for the 800 metres in 2013. Rob said in an interview *'It's a fantastic opportunity to coach somebody like her and I have a responsibility to for Jessica when the 2016 Olympics come round in Rio.*

Rob was born in Billericay on the 23 November 1968 and he attended Furtherwick Park School on Canvey Island.

Robert (Bob) Downs................................... Cyclist

Over the past decade British cycling has been ruling the waves with the likes of Sir Chris Hoy, Sir Bradley Wiggins, Mark Cavendish, Chris Frome, Victoria Pendleton and Laura Trott but where did it all start. Could it have been with our Bob Downs who during the 1980s became a force to be reckoned with. At the time it was considered the golden age of British cycling and Bob was one of the best.

Figure 79 Bob Downs

Bob was born in Basildon on 24 July 1955 and the family lived at No 1 King Edward Road, Laindon moving later to Buller Road, Laindon. He attended Markhams Chase School (now Janet Duke) and Yvonne Edwards tells me that they used to catch the bus for school at Pelhams sweet shop in Laindon High Road. At the tender age of 22 he won the prestigious Gran Premio della Liberazione. This being a single day road race held in Italy annually on the 25 April since 1946. It marks the 1945 fall of Benito Mussolini's Italian Social Republic. Following one of his major wins in the Sealink International in 1980, he went on to represent Great Britain in the 1980 Moscow Olympics in the 100 Kilometres Team Trial in which the team came 9th but in the 1982 Commonwealth Games he won gold in the 100 Kilometres Team Trial with Malcolm Elliott, Joe Waugh and Steve Lawrence.

In 1976 he came 3rd in the British Cycling Premier Calendar Road Race series. This is a season long competition run by British Cycling. It comprises of Road races for the country's top domestic road riders. In 1981 he went two places better and won the competition. Also in 1981 he came 4th in the Milk Race, known today as the Tour of Britain, as he had come second in stages 8 and 11. He also came 4th the following year. Then in 1984 he won the Tour of Ireland.

During his career he rode for the following teams: GS Strada, Manchester Wheelers Club and ended up with Percy Bilton Team 1984/1989 when he turned professional.

Mark Foster..............…......................Swimmer

Although retired, Mark is probably our best known swimmer and possibly our most successful swimmer to date and yes he was born in the Borough in the district of Billericay on 12 May 1970. Sheila his mother saw

Figure 80 Mark Foster

Mark's early promise in the water and took him to a swimming club near their

home in Billericay, but by the time he was two the family had moved to Southend and it was at Warrior Square Pool, Southend that he had his first swimming lesson

Although he admits *"I was lucky enough to really enjoy the whole training process. It was painful sometimes to have to get into the pool at 5am but my approach was to remember I was doing it with all these other kids who were my friends and we just had a good laugh."* There were times though when he could be rather lazy and probably not train as he should have, was this why he never managed an Olympic Gold?

He went to Alleyn Court Preparatory School, Westcliff-on-Sea and Southend High School for Boys where he excelled at athletics, football and tennis. He then went on to the University of Bath.

Marks speciality was short course swimming (25 Metre Pool) and at the age of 15 became the fastest swimmer in the country. His main strokes being freestyle and Butterfly.

He was initially taught by Ann Hardcastle in the pool at Southend-on-Sea. Ann was the mother of Sarah Hardcastle who also became an international swimmer.

He made the British team in 1985 and competed in the 1986 Commonwealth Games in Edinburgh. In 1989 he won his first bronze, as part of the 50 metre freestyle relay in Edinburgh but he said his first real sporting moment came when he won bronze in the 50 metre freestyle in a time of 23.16 seconds at the Commonwealth Games in Auckland in 1990.

The 1990s became a very successful period for him as he broke the World Short Course freestyle record four times, the World Short Course twice and the World Long Course record in a time of 24.07 seconds in 1996.

Throughout his impressive three decade career, Mark won 47 international medals; competed in 5 Olympics, been 8 times Commonwealth champion, 11 times European champion and 8 times World record holder. He trained for a time with 'The Race Club' in Florida, the camp had been founded by two ex-Olympic Swimmers and designed to serve as a training camp for elite swimmers across the world in preparation for Olympics.

His biggest disappointment came when he was not selected to represent Great Britain in the 2004 Olympic Games. He had won the British Olympic Trials 50 metres freestyle in 22.49 seconds, well under the Olympic Qualifying time but seven hundredths outside the time set by the British Standard National Team Director.

He hit back with a gold medal in the World Short Course

Championships in Indianapolis later in the year, in a time of 21.58 seconds in the 50 metre freestyle.

Then at the age of 35 in April 2006 following the European Short Course Competition he decided to retire, though he continued to race in invitation events. But in 2007 he decided to come out of retirement to have a last crack at an Olympic Gold. In the lead up to the games he won silver in the 50 metre freestyle at the 2008 FINA short Course World Competition. At this particular Championship just seconds before the start of the 50 metre freestyle, the zip on Mark's swimsuit broke. It is the sort of mishap that could throw the concentration and scupper the performance of a lesser athlete, but Mark stripped down to his trunks, dived in and swam 21.31, winning a silver medal and, in doing so, qualifying for his fifth Olympic Games. He was honoured with carrying the flag for Great Britain in the opening ceremony during the Parade of Nations.

It turned out he did not even make the semi-final. It is a complete mystery why he never managed to win an Olympic medal and it must also be a mystery to him as well. Whatever he is still one of the greatest swimmers Britain has produced. As expected he retired from swimming for the second time.

Since retiring we frequently see Mark on the television. He has appeared on Countdown, Question of Sport, Dine with me, Celebrity Master chef, Celebrity Juice for Sports Relief Special, member of the 'The Olympians' for let's dance for Sports Relief. Through the key-hole and there have been many others.

In 2008 he appeared in Strictly Come Dancing, being voted off in round six but he followed this up by appearing in the Strictly Dancing arena tour in 2012 dancing with Natalie Lowe. This appears to have resulted in him forming 'Fitsteps' a Dance fitness programme with strictly professionals Natalie Lowe and Ian Waite. It was launched in January 2014.

He has never lost his passion for swimming and in May 2013 he set up the Mark Foster Swimming Academy, ages 11-17.

It was possible his partnership with Clare Balding representing the 2012 Olympics from the aquatic centre made him a household name and more recently, Mark's expertise and personable manner saw him co-hosting the Swimming World Championships 2013 with Gabby Logan and Rebecca Adlington live from Barcelona and he has also been appearing on the Clare Balding Show.

He has not let charities slip by and is patron of the Anaphylaxis

Campaign, a UK charity for people with severe allergies. He won £10,000 for the campaign by participating in 'Who wants to be a Millionaire'.

He is only in his mid-forties so there is no doubt we will see more of his smiling face in the future.

Jillean Hipsey (nee Porter)...............Netball Queen

Jillean was born in 1948 and lived in Pound Lane, Laindon until she was fifteen when the family moved to Berry Lane, Langdon Hills, following compulsory purchase by the Basildon Corporation.

Figure 81 Jillean Hipsey. Ken Porter's collection

She married Peter Hipsey at St Nicholas Church in 1972 after meeting him at a cricket dinner at Bradwell-on-Sea with her brother a few years earlier.

Her first school was Markhams Chase Junior School (now Janet Duke). It was not long before her sporting ability shone through. Although her initial success was on the athletic field, she was never beaten at junior, senior or district school levels over the 60 or 100 yard races and long jump.

It was netball though that she preferred, first playing for the school team in 1958 when she was only ten. The following year she was school captain and her cousin Anne Pope joined her in the team. On passing the eleven plus, she went to Fryern Grammar School, Basildon and continued to shine on the athletic field, hockey field and netball court. It was while competing in the district sports that Jim Peters the marathon athlete approached her parents with the possibility of coaching her. Unfortunately the offer was never taken up.

On leaving school at 17 she joined Fryerns old student's netball team, unfortunately the team folded a few years later. So with another ex-student Chris Laundy (nee Smedley) they formed the Laindon Netball Club which played its home games at Laindon Road School.

This team ran for many years and were a force to be reckoned with locally and in the Anglia region. The team finally hung up its boots about 25 years ago.

Jillean was fortunate to work for a travel agency in London who

Figure 82 Trinidad Games. Ken Porter's collection

allowed her time off for Netball duties for which she has always been very grateful.

It was not long before she found herself playing for the Civil Service at Lincolns Inn Fields where she was approached by Margaret Curtis who had been sent along to watch her play. She asked her to play for the New Campbell side from Dagenham. So at eighteen she was now playing for three sides, Laindon, Civil Service and New Campbell.

Although people were telling Jillean how good she was, she was a comparatively late starter to the game at competitive level. She was twenty-two before deciding to attend county trials. She was selected for the 2nd X1 at Goal Attack and the following year promoted to the 1st X1 as Centre and it was not long before she was appointed Captain. At the same time she found herself captaining the Eastern Region.

It took another seven years and four attempts before she became part of the England Squad; a complete mystery to her peers, who consider her to be one of the top players in the country. On her first England tour to the West Indies in 1978 was nominated Player of the Tournament by the Trinidad Netball Association. In that season too, she received the trophy awarded by the England Coach, to the player who has given most to the game, receiving the trophy again in 1980.

The same year, 1978 she was chosen as Basildon Sports Personality of the Year. Keith Pont the Essex cricketer presented her with the cup at the Carreras clubhouse.

In 1979 she was back in Trinidad for the 5th World Tournament, appointed vice Captain and the following year Captain. She toured Australia and New Zealand in 1981, followed by the 6th World Netball Tournament in Singapore in 1983.

By now Jillean was getting plenty of press in the Netball and Sport Magazines, this is what one of them had to say in 1982: -

'Put together a netball player of enormous talent and enthusiasm, a dedicated, hardworking leader and a woman with a warm, friendly manner and zest for life – then you have some idea of the personality of England's current netball captain, Jillean Hipsey'.

The article finished with:-

'To players and captains of all ages my advice is, 'Go and see Jillean in action – you cannot fail to be impressed and learn from her application and style'.

Also in 1982, she became one of the Evening Echo/Basildon Tyres Sports Personalities of the Month. She received her award from Basildon Tyres sales manager Mick Bradley at Basildon SavaCentre Store. While there she took the opportunity to study the new batch of Tate and Lyle Sugar Bags that carried her picture and favourite recipe. All part of a sponsorship deal agreed between the British Sugar Bureau and the England Netball Association. Jillean donated her reward of £50 to Laindon Netball team to go towards new kit.

Jillean also worked very hard as an ambassador off the court as well as on it. In 1984 she did radio and television interviews with Ron Pickering. With Channel 4 she did a programme on netball, whereby they came and watched her train. She was reserve for the Super stars programme on the television but her real fame came when Ian Botham could not remember her name in the picture quiz on Question of Sport and thought she played for Scotland. (He has been a big disappointment to the family ever since).

1987 saw Jillean playing in her last World Tournament in Glasgow and at the end of the tournament she retired from International Netball at the tender age of 38. Her last game was against the old enemy Australia, to whom they lost, it was her 100th cap. There is no doubt she could have continued and they wanted her to but she felt it was time to go, it was a very emotional occasion with many of her family there.

Figure 83 Ken Porter's collection

She was presented with a gold 'netball and chain' from the President of the AENA (All England Netball Association), Pat Taylor. The supporters showered her with 150 red and white roses, bottles of bubbly, a cake and various other presents and cards. There should have been 150 red and white balloons but unfortunately they went down over night – her response was: - *'What a shame, but I guess that the Trinidad and New Zealand teams would not have appreciated playing the final tiptoeing among 150 balloons'!*

She was fully aware that her husband Peter who was her greatest 'stalwart', was very proud of her successes and was always there to encourage her when times were difficult. She admits she could not have done it without him. He was the leader of the fans and at times wore some outrageous union jack clothing.

Although Peter was from Burnham-on-Crouch and they initially lived at South Woodham Ferrers after getting married before moving Mayland. Laindon was still their sporting home. Peter was well known in the cricketing circles of Laindon. He captained the Laindon Cricket Club for many years. Unfortunately the side folded about fifteen years ago.

Her main position was always centre; she started for England at centre and finished at centre but in between played goal or wing attack. She played where ever the coach wanted her.

She continued to play for Essex for a few more years but her knees started to cause problems so now she concentrates only on coaching her club,

New Campbell, and playing for any of the club's teams that are short from the first to the fourths, not bad for a sixty eight year old. Jillean had many requests to take up coaching and managerial positions within the International set-up but she felt it was time to give a little more time to her home life.

Australia and New Zealand have, for the last forty odd years, been the giants of the game and in all Jillean's time, they beat Australia only once in 1981 and drew with New Zealand in 1985. So to beat both of them since her retirement is a great achievement but of course the England team is now professional whereas in Jillean's time it was still an amateur sport.

Figure 84 Playing Goal Attack, though her main position was centre. Ken Porter's collection

She appeared in the Guinness Book of Records, the first time in 1986 with a picture as the most capped England Player. Not bad for a person who did not come up through the conventional route of the various youth squads but then she was not a conventional player, she took the game to a new level.

Finally in May 2015 Jillean was inducted into the England netball 'Hall of Fame" and in July was awarded the London and South East Regional 'Golden Globe Award for Unsung Hero's' and at the National Finals in September 2015 was made an Honorary Life Member of the England Netball Associations.

Now in her semi-retirement from Netball she has taken up Golf and plays at Burnham-on-Crouch Golf Club with Peter and as you can imagine her trophy cupboard is now filling up with Golf Trophies.

In netball circles Jillean was a legend in her own time. Oh! By the way if you have not guessed I'm her brother.

Stuart Bingham........Basildon's World Champion

Figure 85 Stuart Bingham

For how many years did we sit in front of the television and watch, Ray Reardon, Terry Griffiths, Alex Higgins, Steve Davis, Stephen Henry and in the latter years Jimmy White and Ronnie O'Sullivan win the World Championship. Well we now have our own snooker player to watch, Stuart Bingham who was brought up in Vange, Basildon and went to Swan Mead Infant and Junior School (now Cherry Tree Primary) before moving on to Barstable School.

Stuart was born in Basildon on the 21st May 1976 and following his early years in Vange his family moved to Hockley Road off Long Riding and it was at the nearby Commodore Pub at Stacey's Corner (no longer there, demolished to make way for more residential housing) that he first started to play snooker with his brother and friends.

At the age of seven his parents bought him a 6ft x 3ft snooker table and though he played most ball sports he was hooked on snooker. His most vivid early memory was the 1985 World Championship when Dennis Taylor clawed his way back to beat the favourite Steve Davis who at the time was the world number 1 and had won the previous three finals. It's not surprising though that one of Stuart's snooker heroes while growing up was Steve Davis because of his dominance but he also adds Jimmy White because of his flair.

He played football for Beech United under 12s in the Thundermite League for two years until a knee problem finished his footballing career. He won a league medal with the club which at the time played at Westlake Park, Bowers Gifford. The coach at the time was Martin Fry who is the current organist at St Nicholas Church. Laindon. Martin was also the music teacher at Barstable School when Stuart was there. Martin is still with Beech United but he is now the treasurer.

It was at the Commodore Pub that he was spotted by the manager Dave Meads. He turned professional in 1995 but was still able to play in the IBSF World Snooker Championships (World Amateur Snooker) in 1996 and 1997. Winning in 1996 against Stan Gorski but becoming runner up in 1997 to Marco Fu. It is this defeat that still rankles him, he was 7-1 up only to lose 11-10.

Then for the next decade he was just making up the numbers on the professional circuit although he reached the quarter-final of the Welsh Open in 1999 beating world champion John Higgins in the process. Then in 2000 he caused a major upset by beating Stephen Hendry 10-7 in the first round of the World Championship when ranked only 97 but his form was up and down, however it slowly improved and in the 2006/7 season he broke into the top 32 in the world rankings at number 24.

In the first round of the 2009 World Championship he went out 10-5 to Ronnie O'Sullivan who he believes is the best player he has ever played. However the following year in the UK Championships he defeated Ronnie 9-6, then Marco Fu 9-2 before losing to Northern Ireland's Mark Allen 9-7.

Eventually in July 2011 he won his first world ranking event after sixteen years when he beat Mark Williams 9-8 in the Australian Goldfields Open. To get there he had defeated, Ding Junhui, Mark Allen and former World Champion Shaun Murphy. He slipped up and down the rankings but at the end of the year ranked number 16.

In 2012/13 although his best year to date it was still an up and down year as he won a number of tournaments but also lost out in many others after overcoming such players as Peter Ebdon, Ken Doherty and Mark Selby. He bounced back to form at the end of the season by reaching the final of the Welsh Open only to lose the match 8-9 to Stephen Maguire, but by the end of the season he had jumped 10 places in the world rankings to number six, he had now become someone to be reckoned with.

2013 was another big year for Stuart as he married his partner Michelle (nee Shabi) in a ceremony in Cyprus. The couple have a son (Shae) who was born in 2011. Stuart also has a stepdaughter (Tegan).

The 2013/14 season you could say was similar to the previous with highs and lows, he started off going out fairly early in his first two competitions but bounced back by reaching the semi-finals of the non-ranking Six-red World Championship, losing out to Neil Robertson 7-4. A few more early exits but then as the 2012 Premier League Snooker winner he was invited to join as one of the 16 players to compete in the Champions of Champions tournament in November. On his way to the final he defeated Ricky Walden, Judd Trump and Mike Selby before losing out to Ronnie O'Sullivan 8-10 in the final.

He then reached the semi-final of the 2013 UK Championship his highest position to-date, beating Anthony McGill, David Morris and revenge over Ronnie O'Sullivan before falling foul of Neil Robertson in a thrilling match 8-9. The rest of the season was again up and down though he did win the minor-ranking Dongguan Open in China seeing off Liang Wenbo 4 -1 but his season finished badly with defeat by Ken Doherty in the first round of the World Championship.

The 2014/15 season started off slowly but he then beat Mark Allen 10-3 to win his second ranking title, Shanghai Masters. Then in October 2014 he won the Haining Open defeating Oliver Lines 4-0.

In January 2015 he chalked up his third success of the season by beating Mark Davis 3-2 winning the Championship League at Crondon Park, Stock, Essex. He went on to say that it was nice to win an Essex based tournament. "It is only 20 minutes' drive for me. It is good playing just down the road and I play golf there so it will be nice to go back and remember my win there in the coming weeks."

In an interview for the local Echo newspaper following this win he said that he believes he has another 10 years left at the top of the game and he is not finished yet....well it wasn't long before he proved that.

He failed to reach quarter finals in the Welsh and China Open but then in May he caused a major upset by winning the World Championship.

He was a 50–1 outsider at the start of the tournament but he went on to beat Robbie Williams 10–7 in the first round, Graeme Dott 13–5 in the second round, Ronnie O'Sullivan 13–9 in the quarter-finals, Judd Trump 17–16 in the semi-finals, and Shaun Murphy 18–15 in a thrilling final to win the first world title of his 20-year professional career. At the age of 38, Bingham became the oldest first-time world champion since Walter Donaldson in 1947, and the oldest player to win the title since Ray Readon in 1978.

As you can imaging headlines came thick and fast:
'Stuart Bingham shocks Shaun Murphy in World Snooker Championship Final – The

Guardian.'
'Stuart Bingham wins Snookers World Championship final at the Crucible with victory over Shaun Murphy – TheTelegraph.'
'Bingham bags Crucible title – Sporting Life.'

In a press conference afterwards this is what he had to say:

"It's unreal," "At 15-15 I thought my chance was gone, my arm felt like someone else's and the nerves had got to me."

"You dream of it as a kid playing and practising when you start out, but it's a reality now."

"I was so overwhelmed just to get into the final. Just to witness the final and experience it was great, I didn't care if I won or lost."

He had not clocked he was over the winning line in the final frame, until spectators reacted.

"The crowd clapped and then I looked at the score and realised. I thought I needed another red and colour," he said in his press conference.

"It's unbelievable to be sitting here as world champion."

The local Echo head line read: 'Stu still can't come to terms with the fact that he is the world champion', and he reported to the Echo 'It has been mad. I haven't stopped yet but I have loved it...people have hooted at me in cars and fellow parents at school congratulated me.'

By winning the World Championship Stuart not only pocketed £300,000 prize money, purchased the Final snooker table for £6,400, voted World Snooker player of the year and the writer's player of the year and elevated from 10 in the world rankings to number two, which secured a place for the forthcoming World Cup, partnering with Mark Selby.

Stuart was soon back at his club Rayleigh Lanes Snooker and Social Club to see his fans who had gathered late into the night to watch and cheer Stuart on to win the Championship. The fans as you can imagine were delighted to see his win and this is what some of them had to say:

"We were all there watching and were cheering every shot that went in"

"I think he's always had it in him to be able to do something like this but this is definitely the best I have ever seen him play"

"It was brilliant if he could win because he's a really great geezer as well"

"He's down to earth, he's not above his station and he's very approachable too"

Within days of returning home Stuart was out helping local charities, he visited Choice discount store on Basildon Mayflower Retail Park and showed off his skills on a miniature table. Choice is where his mum Maureen had worked for 23 years and the director of Choice donated £500 towards Stuart's chosen charities, St Luke's Hospice, Basildon and Little Havens Hospice. Next, who work with choice also donated £500 to a charity for disadvantaged youngsters.

Now the question is will he be around in ten years' time as he predicts, I have a feeling he could well be, he has the Basildon spirit.

Oh! He has just been given the Freedom of the Borough of Basildon (2016) along with Mat Whitlock.

Terry Marsh ……..…..........The Fighting Fireman

Figure 86 Terry Marsh

Terry was born on the 7 February 1958, in Stepney into a typical East End family Maisie and Jimmy Marsh and was the third of four children all boys. His dad Jimmy had done a bit of boxing and in fact had won a schoolboy title. Terry tells us in his book 'Undefeated' that his father's other claim to fame is that he had lived in Stepney for forty eight years and unlike others he never knew either of the Kray twins.

By the time he was nine years old Terry had become a champion but not in boxing but at chess of all games when he became the East London Chess Champion and to prove it was no fluke became the London Champion.

On passing his eleven plus he became a pupil of Westminster City Grammar all boy's school, one of the top London schools at the time. He had also joined St Georges boxing club, not because he was necessarily interested in boxing but because it was near to where he lived. As it turned out he lost his first couple of matches which no doubt spurred him on.

Following a change of job for his father the family moved to Pitsea, a move that Terry was more than happy with. The new home had a garden, 4 bedrooms, a dining room, a sunroof, a large fitted kitchen and two toilets which must have been a real luxury compared to their London home which probably was not much better than the old Plotland buildings of the Basildon area.

Although he was never really happy at the Westminster School it must have been a bit of a shock to be enrolled into Chaveldon the local comprehensive school. It did not take him long to settle in and compared to the grammar school the lessons were lax, the discipline devoid and the teachers tender.

It was not long before he was hitting the local Basildon Evening Echo headlines with 'Pitsea boy Heroes in Mercy Dash Drama'. He and a couple of lads had been scavenging for bicycle parts on Pitsea Tip when one got badly cut by glass. The lad that was injured spent several days in hospital and on his release joined Terry to pick up three bikes from a reader who had taken pity on them. However two of the bikes ended up on Pitsea tip as they did not help their street cred.

It did not take long before Terry's dad was making enquiries for a local boxing club so he soon found himself at the Blue House Amateur Boxing Club.

His first fight was against a lad from a Southend Club, he managed to win a unanimous decision and he found himself in the Basildon Echo again.

Boxing was now his life and it was not long before he re-joined his old club even though it meant a lot of travelling. He won the 15/16 Junior ABAs (Amateur Boxing Association) then at sixteen in his final year at school he won the National Schoolboys Championship, followed up by winning the Class B Junior ABAs.

It was time to leave school and he found a job with William Hill bookmakers as a trainee settler. However with a lack of recognition by the boxing authorities he started to get bored with boxing and was missing training. His appetite returned after a couple of fights and an unexpected defeat and at the age of seventeen he was now considered a senior. It was not long before he got his first international call up for the under 19s.

He joined the Royal Marines, serving in Cyprus and in Crossmaglen in Northern Ireland during the troubles. During his time with the Marines he represented the Royal Navy Boxing team and became the 1978 ABA Lightweight Champion, 1980 ABA Welterweight Champion and again in 1981. Also in 1981 he won Gold in the Multi-Nations – Manila. This turned out to be his final year as an amateur.

Just before leaving the Marines he enrolled at Basildon College to further his education by studying for 'O' levels in Maths, English, Physics, Electronics and Chemistry as he had made a decision that he wanted to be an officer in the Marines.

This ambition soon changed when a new boxing manager and

promoter on the block Frank Warren made contact and soon afterwards Terry signed initially with Kieron Murphy but later with Frank Warren. His professional career was about to begin.

It was soon after this that Terry married Jacqui (Bethel) who he had met several years earlier while in the Marines. Within two weeks they had been given a two bedroom flat in Pitsea, the same area that Terry had grown up in during his teenage years.

His first professional fight and win was in October 1981 against Andrew De Costa and twelve fights later he was crowned Southern Area Light-Welterweight after defeating Vernon Vanriel for the vacant title. By now Terry was working for the Fire Brigade and stationed at Tilbury and had become known as the 'Fighting Fireman'.

In September 1984 at the Britannia Leisure Centre, Shoreditch he defeated Clinton McKenzie to take the British Light-Welterweight title. The following year in October 1985 he won the vacant European Light-Welterweight title by defeating the Italian Alessandro Scapecchi in Monte Carlo; he won with a knockout in the seventh round. He defended this title in two further contests in January 1986 and April 1986.

On the 4 March 1987 he took on the American, Joe Manley for the International Boxing Federation (IBF) World Light-Welterweight title. The fight took place in a large marquee (Circus tent) in the car park of Festival Hall, Basildon as Basildon did not have a venue large enough. Marsh won a technical knockout in the tenth round. ITN commentators hailed it *as "one of the best British victories seen in a long time"*. Next day he returned to work at the Fire Station.

As you would expect he became a national celebrity and offers of TV appearances and interviews came flooding including episode of "This is Your Life" with Eamonn Andrews who presented him with the 'famous red book'.

Then a few months later, 1 July, he defended the title at the Royal Albert Hall, Kensington against Japanese, Akio Kameda, winning again by a technical knockout, this time in the seventh round.

By now Terry knew that he was suffering from epilepsy so he decided to retire and did so as the undefeated IBF World Champion. He has always maintained that he intended to retire irrespective of the epilepsy. In the late 1980's a local Leisure Centre in Pitsea was named after him, unfortunately subsequent squabbles between local councillors saw it being renamed the Eversley Leisure Centre. For a time the mosaic plaque at the centre in his honour was still on display but it has since been removed and surprisingly nobody knows where it is.

Soon after his retirement he opened up a betting shop in Romford with his brothers and at a later date, a second one. Although he did not spend a considerable amount of time in them as he had plenty of media and promotional work to keep him busy.

But unfortunately his marriage to Jacqui had been to say the least very volatile and they eventually split up. Around the same time he was quarrelling with Frank Warren over a number of issues and on the 30 November 1989 somebody shot him and because there was an ongoing libel case between them, Terry became a chief suspect. Two months later Terry was arrested and charged with the attempted murder of Frank Warren. He spent the next ten months in prison before he was subsequently acquitted.

The libel case eventually went to trial with neither party being found guilty it was Terry's word against Frank's word. By now Terry and Jacqui had divorced.

After all this one would have thought that Terry would like a quiet life, but no he has worked as a stock broker, self-published an autobiography titled "Undefeated", and stood in several elections for UK Parliament. In the 2010 election he stood as independent candidate in the seat of South Basildon and East Thurrock. He had changed his name by deed poll to "None of the above X" as a protest against there being no option to select "None of the above" on the ballot paper. He stood again in the 2015 elections. His reasoning was that the system does not allow people to express dissatisfaction with the candidates on the ballot paper. Needless to say he did not win either.

Previously in the 1997 election he had stood as a Lib Dem but had to withdraw after he was charged with fraud regarding two student grants after going back to university after the end of his boxing career. Again he was cleared of any wrong doing.

Well I thought that was it, what a life, what a career undefeated in the ring and undefeated in the courts. A true character but then he pops up again this time in the new sport of Chess Boxing.

Chess Boxing is as you would expect a combination of chess and boxing. It was devised by a Dutch performance artist, Lepe Rubingh. It involves the competitors fighting in alternating rounds of chess and boxing. The first competition took place in Berlin in 2003. The competitors win the contest by:-
Knockout (Boxing rounds)
Technical Knockout (Boxing rounds)
Checkmate (Chess rounds)

Exceeding of the time limit by opponent (Chess rounds), Etc.

Terry's first match was held on Saturday 14 June 2014 at the Scala, Kings Cross where he defeated Chris Powell in round nine by checkmating his opponent – still undefeated.

He had over 200 fights, 27 being professional, 26 wins and one draw. He has three children, Kelly, Karl and Gabrielle and still lives in the Basildon area.

His book 'Undefeated' is a really good read and as you would expect he pulls no punches.

George Sawyer.........Hydroplane Record Breaker.

The Daily Express on Saturday October 18 1986 reported on the Power Boat record week that was taking place on Lake Windermere:-

'More than 25 National Records have been smashed and there can be few more unlikely-looking speed kings than 58 year old Essex builder George Sawyer.

At 6ft.4in and 16 stone, it is miracle he can fit in a pencil thin hydroplane. But as the early mist rose from the still lake, he sliced through the water like a diamond on glass, shattering the National 700cc pump hydroplane record, by 21 m.p.h. with an average speed of 103.87 m.p.h.'

Then on the Thursday the local Evening Record reported: -

'Veteran power boat driver George Sawyer, of Basildon today became the first 100 mph plus record breaker of this year's Power Boat Records attempts week on Lake Windermere.

George, 58, the oldest competitor, sped over the lake at an average of 103.87 mph to break his own national record for OD Pump Hydroplane of 700cc.

Yesterday he broke it with a speed of 96 mph, an amazing increase on the previous record of 74.37 mph.

George, who is a building contractor at Langdon Hills, said "I have been completing on Windermere since the very first power boat week in 1971." '

George was born in Worthing Road, Laindon in 1928. He initially went to Dunton Junior School, transferring to Markhams Chase Junior School (now Janet Duke's) when the family moved along the road closer to the Laindon High Road. He then went to Laindon High Road School before moving on to Mid Essex Technical School, Chelmsford to study engineering.

In 1945 he volunteered and joined the Royal Armoured Corp. seeing service in Italy, Palestine and Gaza before being demobbed in 1948.

He formed his own joinery company at Hullbridge in the early 1950s.

Nina his wife has supported her husband George in his endeavours ever since.

Figure 87 George Sawyer

During the early 1940s he joined the Laindon Athletic Club and the Southend District Motor Cycle Club in the 1950s. In 1962 he took up Hydroplane racing, It was members of the Motor Cycling club that got him involved in power boats by inviting him to Gosfield Lake, near Braintree and pushed him into a boat to have a go. He was hooked and came away having bought the boat. He learnt to drive at Gosfield and Grangewater, South Ockendon and within weeks he had his first National race, at Oulton Broad, Suffolk.

In October 1982 he broke the Hydroplane Class OE and Formula 3 – 850cc one kilometre world record on Lake Windermere with a speed of 100.291 mph. This was followed up by him being made a member of the K7 club, formed by Donald Campbell for people who have succeeded in setting a speed record over 100mph on water.

To the relief of Nina, George eventually gave up racing in 1995 (aged 67) and he admits it a very dangerous sport and has seen two friends die in the water in 1988 and 1992. George said in an interview with the Echo in 2010 that it is the lightness of the boats weighing on average about 120kg, which makes them so treacherous and if the boat nose dives into the water it stops dead and smashes. Most famously, this kind of crash caused the death of champion racer Donald Campbell in 1967, while he raced his hydroplane Bluebird K7.

His scariest momentcame in 1973 when he fell in some difficult water. He thought to himself I will pop up in a moment, but nothing happened, he was trapped under a fellow racer's boat. While Nina was panicking the other fellow had thought George had been cut to shreds by his boat's propeller. When he did pop up his friend said 'George is that you?' and he replied 'of course it's me who do you think it is?'

One of his greatest disappointments in recent years was the closing of the Boat Museum at Wat Tyler Park, Pitsea, Basildon a few years ago. At its

Figure 88 By Kind permission of George Sawyer

peak there were 50 boats and 100 engines of all types on display and George and Nina were members of the Friends of the Museum. Both George and Nina are still active members of the Essex Hydroplane Racing Club. In their spare time they travel Britain and the continent in their camper van.

Figure 89 Nina receiving the RYA award from Princess Anne. By kind permission of George Sawyer

In 1988 they moved round the corner into Welbeck Drive, Langdon Hills. I wonder how many people in the road know that they have a champion amongst their midst.

After his retirement from actual racing Hydroplanes he continued to officiate/organise and promote all national and international circuit power boat racing. In 2011 both George and Nina were given the Royal Yacht Association (RYA) award.

Max Whitlock..............................Gymnast

I was well on my way in finishing the book when up popped Max Whitlock. If there is anybody who has put Basildon on the map in recent years it is Max.

He was born at Hemel Hempstead, Hertfordshire on 13 January 1993. He joined the Basildon based South Essex Gymnastic Club now located at the Basildon Sporting Village, Cranes Farm Road, Basildon when he was 12 years old. He has recently moved into the Borough and is living with his girlfriend Leah Hickton another talented gymnast. They have been together for five years after meeting at the club. Max's coach is Scott Hann who just happens to be Leah's brother-in-law.

He attended Nash Mills Primary and Longdean Secondary school, he started swimming at the age of 7 but a friend recommended that he tried gymnastics, he took to it like duck to water, loved it and never looked back. He joined the Sapphire School of Gymnastics in Hemel Hempstead before moving on to the South Essex Gymnastic Club. He trains up to 35 hours a week but still enjoys swimming and watching other Olympic sports, such as athletics.

He first came to the attention of the British Gymnastics Body when he was 9 years old and he joined their World Class programme. It was not until he competed at the Junior European Championship in Birmingham in 2010 that he really started to realise how good he was. He won Gold on the Floor, Gold on the Pommel and a Silver in the All –round competition.

Figure 90 By kind of Richard Wadey

Max's meteoric rise since has seen him win 21 major medals and in

so became the first British man to win a World gymnastic title. His first major success came at the age of seventeen when the England Team won silver in the Commonwealth Games in Delhi, he also won silver on the Pommel Horse and Bronze on the Horizontal Bar.

In the 2014 Commonwealth Games in Glasgow he won team gold, All-round gold, Floor exercise gold, silver on the Pommel Horse and Bronze on the Parallel Bars.

At the European Championship he won team gold at Montpellier in 2012. This was the first time that the British team had won gold in these Championship's beating both Russia and Romania. Then in 2013 in Moscow he won gold for the Floor Exercise, All-around silver and Bronze on the Pommel Horse. A year later in Sofia he went two better on the Pommel Horse by winning gold, beating the 2012 Olympic champion Krisztian Berki, following up with a Team silver.

In his only Olympics to date in London in 2012 he won Bronze on the Pommel Horse behind his rival Louis Smith who took silver. There was also bronze for the team being part of the first British team to win a medal at the Olympics.

It has been in the World Championships where he has really shone. In Antwerp in 2013 he won silver on the Pommel Horse. In 2014 at Nanning he won All-around silver, matching Daniel Keatings best performance by a British gymnast.

2015, after a mediocre start was going to be his year. He competed in the English Championship in March as the defending AAA champion and won gold on the pommel horse. He struggled in his other events and did not compete on the vault. At the British Championship he won silver on the pommel horse behind Louis Smith. After these championships it was found that he was suffering from Glandular Fever but he still had a crack at the European Championships in Montpellier but failed to qualify in any of the finals.

He decided to take a rest from training and public appearances to recover, but in May on social media he announced he was returning to training and within six months he had taken the gymnastic world by storm by winning silver for the Team award, silver for his floor Exercise program and finally gold on the Pommel Horse beating his close rival and friend Louis Smith by .1 of a point.

This is what his coach Scott Hann said in an interview to the Independent: "The aim was always just to make the final and everything else would be a bonus. To win a medal was absolutely incredible. I saw Max after and he had tears in his eyes – it was a really emotional day." He had tears what about the rest of us who were watching it?

In 2014 he was nominated for BBC Sports Personality of the Year which went to Lewis Hamilton. There should be no doubt that he will be nominated again for 2015 and be in with a shout.

Hemel Hempstead are no doubt proud of their young star but Basildon also has a right to claim him as one of theirs as he has trained in the Borough for over ten years and now lives within the Borough no more than 10 minutes from the gym.

Like Stuart Bingham he has just received the Freedom of the Borough of Basildon.

Postscript: Wins gold in the individual floor exercise, two hours later won gold in the individual pommel horse to add to the bronze won in the team all-round gymnastic event at Rio Olympic Games 2016 - Oh! we must not forget his coach - Scott Hann.

Perry McCarthy ....'Mad Dog'

If there was any Basildon Boy or Laindon Boy for that matter who is unique it has to be Perry McCarthy and his motto is "Whatever it takes," and that's the reason I have decided to finish the book with him.

What is so special about him, well his sporting passion was one of the most dangerous sports in the world, he became a Formula One driver but his career was cut short through injury.

His close friend the 1996 World Champion Damon Hill said this of him 'I have constant admiration for how he turns a no hope situation into some sort of triumph'. Following his departure from Formula One he become the first secret racing driver from the BBC Top Gear i.e.: 'The Stig'.

Perry was born on 3 March 1961 in Stepney, East London and the family moved to Dagenham when he was three then on to Stanford-le-Hope where he went to his first school Gifford's Primary in Corringham. His father was a painter and decorator and was doing fairly well so at the age of six the family moved to a new detached house in a cul-de-sac off Church Road opposite the Laindon Police Traffic Garage.

Figure 92 Perry McCarthy. By kind permission of Perry McCarthy

He remembers that the area back in the late 1960s was surrounded by fields. From here he crossed the A127 and walked daily up the hill to his new school 'Laindon Park Junior School.' This was the first Board school to be built in Laindon in 1877. He graduated to Laindon High Road School before going onto Basildon College.

Perry was later to admit that he did not like school and at times could be a mischievous little devil and like many youngster of his age would play 'Knock down Ginger' around the high density Pound Lane Estate just a stone's throw from Laindon High Road School.

However he went on to pass all seven 'O' levels exams and planned to take his A-Levels at sixth form. In his spare time he became a member of the Air Training Corps based in Church Road, Laindon not far from where he was living. He had his own uniform and bugle which he never learnt to play but it convince him that he would pass his A Levels and go to University and then join the Royal Air Force and become a fighter pilot.

His ambition soon changed because after a year at sixth form he became bored and left and got a job with Alliance Shipping. He still did not know what he wanted to do but he knew it was not shipping but after a number of interviews for various roles he decided to go back to college, so he enrolled at Basildon College to study A-courses in Law, Economics, Sociology and Art.

While at college he took his driving test but failed, something to do

Figure 93 Perry working on the oil rigs. By kind permission of Perry McCarthy

with lack of Highway Code knowledge and going too fast but he re-took the test a month later and passed. He promptly went out and bought his first car for £100 'Old Mk 1 Escort'. Although he put this poor old car through its paces he still was not taking much interest in motor racing.

Perry was about 18 when art and a friend at college first whet his appetite for motor racing. His friend gave him a magazine called Grand Prix International (GPI) and he started to draw the cars and it was not long before he started reading about them and its drivers, the likes of Nelson Piquet and Giles Villeneuve. He also started watching the races on the television – he was hooked.

At around this time his father's painting business hit the big time with a contract to help maintain the Oil Rigs in the North Sea, so he went out and bought Perry a Triumph Spitfire sports car. Perry was in his element racing around Basildon, tyres screaming, the top down and listening to Bee Gee's 'Saturday Night Fever'

Figure 94 By kind permission of South Hill Garage, Langdon Hills

Another hobby of his, other than his drawing and driving, was playing the keyboard and for a time he had a part time job working for his friend Bob and the owner of a musical shop in Grays demonstrating instruments. Then one day a chap walked into the shop and spoke to Bob and then went over to Perry and said 'What do you want to do?'

Not having a clue who he was Perry retorted sarcastically 'I'm gonna be a Formula One racing driver.' The response was 'well, you'd better come with me then,' 'My name is Les Ager, I'm an instructor at Brands Hatch and Bobby here tells me you are the best thing since sliced bread.' – Perry was on his way.

The first problem however was finance as motor racing is a very expensive sport and requires a considerable amount of sponsorship. So it was initially back to Dad, but Dad thought he was a b........dy idiot. However he did arrange for Perry to work on the oil rigs as long as he finished his A Levels, so it was the start of a ten years slog to become a Formula One racing driver.

After two years on the rigs doing 12 to 16 hour days and studying he passed his 'A' levels and by crashing motor cars as if they had gone out of fashion. He also spent time knocking on doors of companies and he eventually managed to obtain some initial sponsorship. One of his earliest sponsorships came about by his cousin Gary Denham talking to Volvo dealership South Hill Garage, Langdon Hills, into supplying him with a road car.

He realised that his racing career had to start with Formula Ford 1600 competition but with whom. After watching a couple of races he noticed that a driver called Ayrton Senna was doing particularly well driving for 'Van Diemen'. As it turned out that a team who ran Van Diemen cars were based in Rayleigh just a few miles up the road from where he was living. It turned out that they were looking for another driver, he made contact and was signed on for the last two races of the 1981 'Champion of Brands' series and the Formula Ford Festival World Cup.

Well not only did he achieve pole position in his first race, but he actual won it but surprise, surprise he crashed in the final and then went onto crash again in Festival World Cup. Something he was going to make a habit of over the coming years, no wonder he picked up the nickname of 'Mad Dog'.

Perry stayed with Van Diemen team through the 1982 season and into the start of the 1983 but too many crashes saw Perry move over and join the Rushen Green Racing team. With the final round of the championship Perry was leading by four points but he had a scare when in qualifying his engine cut out and somebody ran into the back of him. The team quickly realigned the damaged rear wheel just in time for him to get in sufficient laps and on his last lap managed to equal the time of Peter Rogers, so they lined up next to each other for the race.

Figure 95 One of Perry's many crashes. By kind permission of Perry McCarthy

Perry went on to win the race and become the 1983 Dunlop Tomorrow Champion as he had won six out of the ten races. So at 22 years of age he was a Champion and awarded the local Evening Echo sports personality of the month.

In 1984 he remained in Formula Ford 1600 but was struggling to get sponsorship but he eventually ended up with a new car from Van Diemen and raced for Motor Racing International. During this year he met up and befriended Mark Brundell.

Unfortunately the car appeared to be under powered and this niggled Perry and at Oulton Park, Cheshire he was in third place trying to keep up with the leaders. He collided with John Booth which resulted in Perry writing his car off and ending up unconscious with a broken back, his worst crash to date and there had been many.

It was during his period of recovery that he met his future wife Karen Waddilove some four years after he had first set eyes on her at Basildon College.

Unlike many racing drivers he had not been involved with karts so for the next five/six years he worked his way through junior categories of motor racing such as Formula Ford 1600, Formula 3, F3000 then eventually in 1991 he was chosen to test drive for Footwork Formula One team but it was not until the beginning of the 1992 season that he signed for the independent Andrea Moda team. He had made it as he was now a Formula One racing driver. On his journey he had met up and become friends with Damon Hill, Johnny Herbert, Martin Donnelly, Julian Bailey and along with Mark Blundell they became known as the 'Rat Pack'.

The team was run by Andrea Sassetti who felt that it would be a good way to advertise his shoe business. The team unfortunately was under financed and completely out of its depth, the car was unreliable and he failed to qualify for any of his ten races. The team folded before the end of the 1992 season and Perry was left without a drive. He did not race in Formula One again although during the 1990s he test drove for Williams and Benetton. In 1990 an interview with the Times dubbed him as 'the world's unluckiest racing driver'.

A disaster, his Formula One career was over before it had really started, but it did not do justice to his talents and it was not long before he started a successful career in racing sports cars. In 1996 he competed with co-drivers in 24 hours of Le Mans driving a Chrysler Viper GT-R but unfortunately engine failure was to force the team out after 96 laps of the 354 lap race. He was to complete another five Le Mans, his most successful being in 1999 driving an Audi R8C and competing 198 laps out of 366 laps before gearbox failure caused the team to retire. His last was in 2003 again in an Audi R8C this time his team mate run out of petrol after only 28 laps.

It was around 2002 that he was approached by his old friend Jeremy Clarkson and Top Gear producer Andy Williams to become the first Top Gear 'Stig'. Perry accepted and a legend was born, he appeared on the show in 2002 and 2003 all dressed in black, racing cars around a track and getting up to all sorts of tricks and the idea was that nobody was to know who the Stig was. He played the game even when he went to the studio canteen as he would keep his leathers and helmet on and speak in a French accent. However Perry got tired of racing around a track week after week sodecided to give up the role. The next Stig was to wear white.

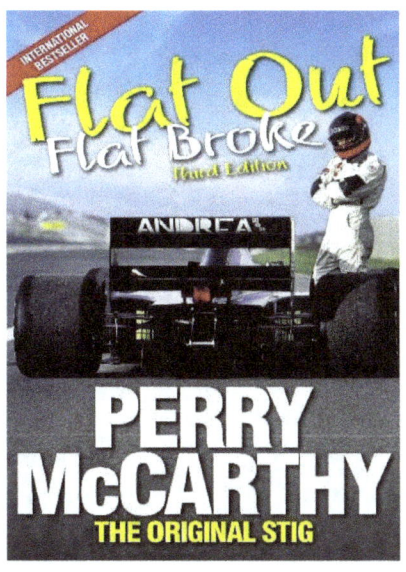

Figure 96 By kind permission of Perry McCarthy

Perry retired from racing in 2004 following a major injury to his left shoulder which made it impossible for him to race but before he did he produced his first book 'Flat Out, Flat Broke' a fascinating read

He pulls no punches on his career, it has been published and republished at least 9 times and it's a must to read.

Perry is no doubt outspoken but comical with it, with amusing impersonations so it is no surprise that he has become a superb speaker and has therefore created a successful, lucrative career as an after-dinner speaker. This has involved him in TV Presenting, Journalism and commentator in addition to his after-dinner speaking.

This has also resulted in him receiving many headlines:
- The Telegraph .....'a new cult hero'
- The America's Sunday Express – 'a comedian locked inside a racing driver's body'
- The London Evening Standard – 'A fantastic funny story' (book of the week).

Paul Gibson records on the Laindon & District community website that Perry was the guest speaker at Basildon Round Table 50th Charter Dinner at the Holiday Inn Basildon in May 2013 and held his audience spellbound for over an hour talking about his life as the Stig and his rise through the ranks from go-carts to Formula One.

Perry still lives with his wife Karen and three daughters in an old farm house on the edge of Billericay.

He finishes his book with 'Although I can't end by saying 'Mad Dog is back', I can tell you that 'Mad' Dog' is on tour and still flat out!

Monaco: Back row from left: Gerhard Berger, Ayrton Senna, Nigel Mansell.
Middle row: Mika Hakkinen, Christian Fittipaldi, me, JJ Lehto, Andrea de Cesaris
Front row: Michael Schumacher, Paul Belmondo, Eric van de Poele, Roberto Moreno,
Pierluigi Martini
(Sutton)

Chapter 7 - That's it – for now!

Well there you have it, fifty individuals who were either born or lived in the Basildon district and have received national or international recognition. However, as mentioned in the introduction there are many more people I could include but I have left them out partly because I would never finish the book or the information is scarce. In addition there are many young people who are slowly making a name for themselves especially in the world of sports and entertainment.

The other individuals I am aware of that have a connection with Basildon: Lee Harrison (Footballer), Josh Cullen (footballer) Brian Horne (Footballer), Lee Barnard (Footballer), Paul Parker (Footballer), Phil Dudley (Footballer). Paul Clark (Footballer), Daniel Bentley (Footballer), Casey Stoney (Footballer), Richard Osman (TV Personality), Kara Tointon (Actress), Bobby Lockwood (Actor), Mike Edmonds (Actor), Gemma Ray (Musician), Jamel Hadjkura (Actor), Daniel Brooks (Golfer), Perry Bamonte (Musician), Richard Moss (Tennis Player), Ollie Fynn (Walker), William Henry Panter (Royal Navy), Nick Logan (Journalist), David Gandy (model), Rico Daniels (The Salvager), Josh Batch (Ice Hockey), Andy Blake (Paralympian), Scott Robinson (Singer – Five), Q boy (Entertainer), Matthew Yates (Athlete), Bill Longmuir (Golfer), Basil Gordon Reitz (Commentator), Caroline Powell (Ice Skater), Jinian Wilde (Singer), Megan Dallas (Singer), Ryan Robertson (Singer), Hollie Barrie (Singer), Brooklyn Lammiman, (Singer), Gerry Slattery (Guitarist) Allan Taylor (Snooker), Zac Surety (Snooker), Alice Green (Squash), Josh Da Silva (Handball), Caroline Powell (Skier), Josh Batch (Ice Hockey), Che Chesterman (Singer), Conner Brown (Baseball) Alison Drake (Athlete), Nicholas Farrell (Actor) and I am sure there are many more.

I must say I probably had only heard of about half of those that I have come across. So I am amazed at the amount of talent that has emerged from Basildon area and therefore wonder if there is other district in the country that has such talented pedigree.

As already mentioned we have Christopher Martin Road so maybe it is time that Basildon Borough Council should start naming its new roads after some more of their famous forefathers who were either born or had a strong connection to the area. Such as Nathaniel Woodard (Educationist), Rev. John Pell, Joan Sims (Carry on Star), Joe Goodman (who made us laugh), Marion Wilberforce (Aviation Queen), Edgar Longstaffe (Victorian Artist), Elizabeth Reade (Puritan) for starter.

Books also by Ken Porter

This book isn't a story it's an historical account of what life was like for the German POW's who spent time incarcerated in Camp 266 at Langdon Hills in Essex. The camp opened just before the end of the Second World War and saw the arrival of its first inhabitants in April 1945 before closing its doors in June 1948. The camp could hold up to 800 prisoners at a time and also had satellite camps at nearby places such as Tillingham and Purfleet.

It includes accounts from some of the prisoners themselves, looking at what they did before the outbreak of war. It then looks at how and where they were captured, their time spent at the camp and what they did after the war on their release.

Some met local girls, fell in love, married and began new lives living in England. Their personal stories along with newspaper articles of the day, prisoners letters as well as other documents, help bring the book to life giving it a truly unique feeling. There are stories from some of the local residents who lived through it all and got to know some of the POW's quite closely. In some cases this included inviting them in to their homes and befriending them. Some of these friendships lasted for years after the war.

Only the passage of time causing some of them to finally succumb.

Read their stories and find yourself transported back in time to a bygone era that was the start of a new beginning for all of us.

Publisher: Affinity Self-Publishing Ltd

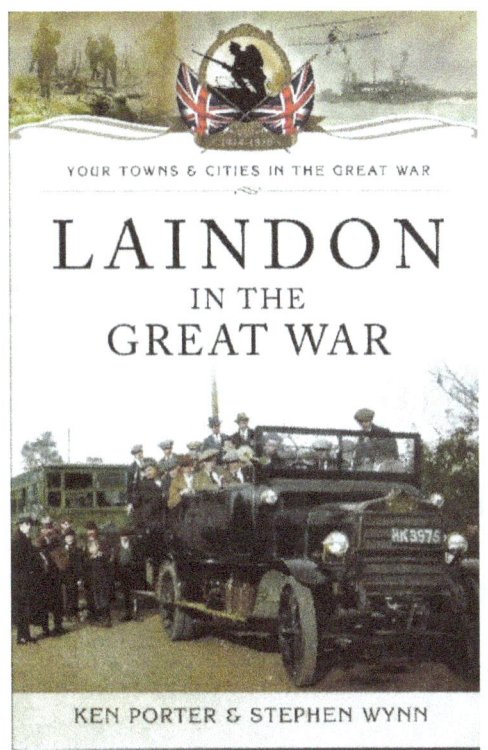

Laindon in the Great War is a detail account of how the war impacted on Laindon and the surrounding district, known today as Basildon, from the outbreak of the Great War in 1914, to the long-awaited peace of 1918.

Throughout the country, initially, there was enthusiasm and excitement for the war, but this soon changed as vivid reports of the war effort began to reach the populous. Fears of invasion and spies around every corner increased, which resulted in a number of locals being reported, in some cases, for very trivial incidents.

While local men fought heroically overseas, two nearby explosives factories provided employment for the town's womenfolk. The book charts the stories of these women, revealing the dangerous conditions of the factories and accidents that entailed. As Laindon was a prominent farming area, despite being located only 20 miles from London, a number of local women, and some from further afield, also joined the Women's Land Army and work laboriously for long hours on the farms.

Included throughout the book are stories of the heroic men who fought on our behalf. The authors present us with individual's memories, passed down through families that bring to life what our men went through and what life was like for those on the home front. The book is a powerful eyewitness account that allows Laindon's wartime citizens, who lived through these momentous and catastrophic events, to tell their own stories in their own words.

Publisher: Pen & Sword

Prior to the outbreak of the Great War in 1914, the Castle Point District was made up of four very quaint, peaceful little parishes: Canvey Island, South Benfleet, Hadleigh and Thundersley. The initial enthusiasm shown by the young men of this area, who were enthusiastic to be part of an adventure that was to be 'over by Christmas', was mirrored by thousands of other courageous young men around Britain. Most understood that it was their sworn duty to stand up for their king and country. They didn't stop to think or even fully appreciate the hardship and fear they would leave behind on the home front.

This book tells of the memories and recollections of some of these brave men who were fortunate enough to return home to their friends and families. For the ones who weren't so luck, we hear from people who endured the pain of a love lost forever more.

Included throughout are a collection of invaluable wartime newspaper reports that recount daily life, telling of the sacrifices that those left behind had to endure whilst reading about the war dead, their numbers increasing on an almost daily basis.

From the extraordinary role of women during the war, the conscientious objectors and those exempt from the fighting, to the aftermath of war when the district celebrated victory while dealing with the painful loss of 189 men, all aspects of wartime Castle Point are covered in this remarkable account, interspersed with a number of wartime poems that further explain in verse what life was like during these dark days.

Publisher: Pen & Sword

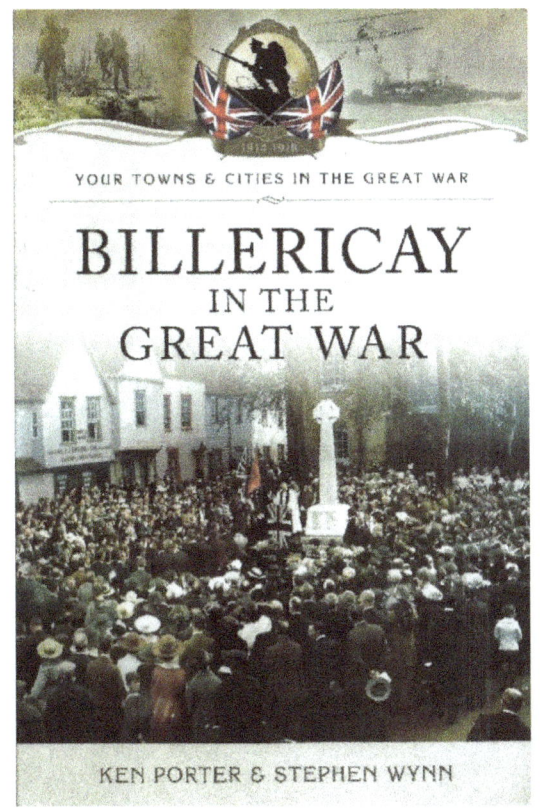

In 1914 Billericay was a peaceful, compact town of around 2,000 inhabitants. The First World War began in August of that year and like the pace of life in the village, it started slowly for the people of Billericay. To start with it was something that they only read about in the newspapers but slowly soldiers started to be billeted in the town. There was an Army camp in Mountnessing Road for the ordinary soldier but the officers were billeted in people's houses. Initially there was excitement and enthusiasm for the war but that soon turned to sorrow and fear as more and more local men were dying on the Western Front.

September 1916 saw a Zeppelin crash in a field at nearby Great Burstead, the burnt and disfigured remains of the German airmen left nobody in doubt just of how real and painful the war was. February 1918 even saw German soldiers come to the town as Prisoners of war, interned in the local Billericay Work House. They were the enemy but not monsters; just ordinary men like those in Billericay who had gone off to fight in a war that they most probably didn't want to be part of. When the war ended and the guns fell silent, men would return to their families to get on with their lives and for the ones who didn't make it back, there would be the commemoration of their names on a war memorial for future generations to remember.

Billericay in the Great War tells the full story of the history of this much loved Essex town from the outbreak of the Great War until peace in 1918 and explains the changes of the town's landscape over that time, as well as the impact the war had on its residents coping with the stresses of war-time rationing and the loss of loved ones.

Complete with over 50 integrated period photographs, this book is

ideal for all military enthusiasts or residents of the surrounding areas.
Publisher: Pen & Sword

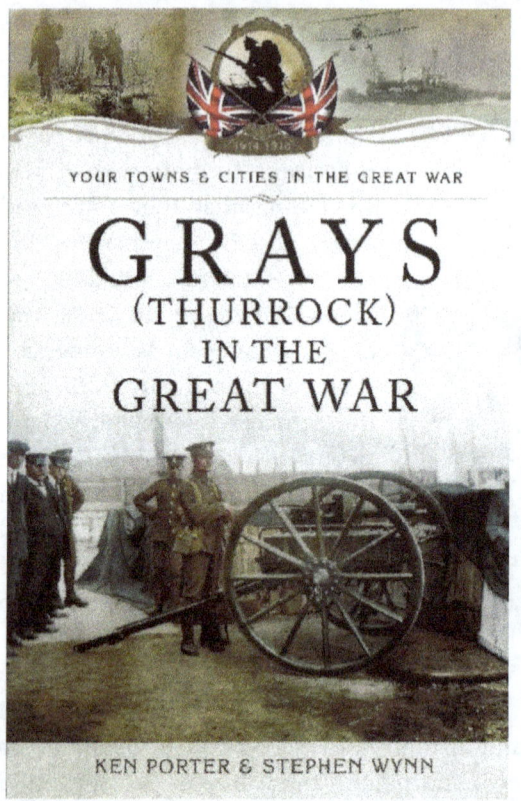

Grays (Thurrock) in the Great War is a detailed account of how the experience of war impacted on the Grays and wider Thurrock area from the outbreak of the Great War in 1914, to the long-awaited peace of 1918. Between these years, the nearby Tilbury Docks played their part in the war but not as a hub of military deployments. The only German prisoner of war to escape from Britain and make it back home to Germany in the Great War passed through the docks, as did a spy who subsequently executed at the Tower of London. Tilbury Fort and Coalhouse Fort at East Tilbury also played an important part in protecting London from a sea bourn invasion, by monitoring shipping on the river Thames to prevent German naval ships from attacking.

With so many men fighting overseas, the Kynochs munitions factory, near Fobbing, became a major source of employment in the area, particularly for women. The site, which produced much-needed ammunitions, became so big that it included its own housing estate, a hospital and a railway line and was eventually referred to as Kynochtown. Soon, Thurrock's people were joined by German prisoners of war, as POW camps developed at Horndon House Farm, Puddledock Farm and Woodhams Quarry in West Thurrock, which housed over 150 German prisoners.

The book documents the tragedies and triumphs of those living in the Grays and Thurrock area and the day-to-day preoccupations of a community seeking to find normality in a reality so far removed from anything they had ever known. Publisher: Pen & Sword

References:

That One Idea - Nathaniel Woodard and his Schools by Leonard and Evelyn Cowie (1991).
Nathaniel Woodard by Sir John Otter (1925)
www.arsenal.com
www.7amkickoff.com/RoguesGallery/StewartRobson
www.Wikipedia
www.graceguide.co.uk/Henry_Selbe-Shaw
www.MarkFoster.co.uk
www.IMBD
www.charlesleatherland.info
www.arsenal.com
www.Notts County-mad-co.uk
www.7amkickoff.com/Roguesgallery/StewartRobson
Sunday Express 30/10/2012
The Guardian – Eastwood stays true to Romany roots.
The Guardian 02/02/2015
Independent 01/04/2005
Basildon Echo
WSC (when Saturday Comes) 196 – June 2003
This is Basildon by Michael Healy
Flat Out, Flat Broke by Perry McCarthy
Portrait of Basildon Plotlands – The Enduring Spirit by Deana Walker
Puritan Origins of North America's First University – dissertation by Tito G Correa
Is anybody out there – Joe Goodman's autobiography
High Spirits (200) by Joan Sims
Just Can't Get Enough (making of Depeche Mode) by Simon Spence
Essex Own by Dee Gordon
www.laindonhistory.org.uk
www.benfleethistory.org.uk
www.hadleighhistory.org.uk

www.ingramcontent.com/pod-product-compliance
Lightning Source LLC
LaVergne TN
LVHW021559070426
835507LV00014B/1863